EARLY WRITINGS

The Collected Works of Norbert Elias

NORBERT ELIAS

Early Writings

Translated by Edmund Jephcott

The Collected Works of Norbert Elias VOLUME 1

Edited by Richard Kilminster

UNIVERSITY COLLEGE DUBLIN PRESS
Preas Choláiste Ollscoile Bhaile Átha Cliath

© Norbert Elias Foundation, Amsterdam, 2002, 2006
German edition published by Suhrkamp Verlag, Frankfurt/Main
as volume 1 of the Norbert Elias Gesammelte Schriften, 2002

Published 2006 by University College Dublin Press
as volume 1 of the Collected Works of Norbert Elias

ISBN 1-904558-39-9

University College Dublin Press
Newman House, 86 St Stephen's Green
Dublin 2, Ireland
www.ucdpress.ie

Cataloguing in Publication data available from the British Library

Typeset in Ireland in Baskerville by Elaine Burberry, Bantry, Co. Cork
Text design by Lyn Davies
Printed in England on acid-free paper
by MPG Books Ltd, Bodmin, Cornwall

CONTENTS

NORBERT ELIAS
1897–1990

Norbert Elias is one of the great sociologists of our time. Born in 1897, he lived through most of the twentieth century, and found his life radically affected by some of that century's major events. Brought up in a Jewish family in the German *Kaiserreich*, he served as a soldier in the First World War, became a sociologist in the short-lived Weimar Republic, had to flee his country after the National Socialists came to power in 1933, suffered hard times as a refugee in Paris and London, and entered on a university career in England only in his late fifties. Having reached retirement age in 1962, he taught sociology in Ghana for two years, and, after his return to Europe, remained active for more than 25 years writing and teaching in various countries. He died in Amsterdam in 1990, at the age of 93.

Elias's protected youth in the Silesian city of Breslau – then in Germany, now Wrocław in Poland – came to an abrupt end when he enlisted to serve in the German army during the First World War. Following his demobilisation, Elias studied medicine and philosophy at the University of Breslau. He wrote his doctoral thesis in philosophy, graduating in 1924, but not before having become highly critical of what he saw as the philosophers' failure to recognise the importance of the creation and transmission of knowledge as an intergenerational learning process, and ultimately rejecting philosophy as a discipline. The runaway inflation of 1922–3 forced him to take work for a time in business, and when he returned to his studies he chose the nascent discipline of sociology at the University of Heidelberg. He worked under Alfred Weber, Max's brother, but also became associated with the young Karl Mannheim who was establishing his reputation in the sociology of knowledge. In 1930 Mannheim moved to a chair at Frankfurt, and Elias joined him as his Assistant in the Department of Sociology, members of which shared a milieu with the Marxist 'Frankfurt School' but remained intellectually and organisationally separate.

At Frankfurt, Elias wrote his *Habilitationsschrift* (the thesis that qualified him for a career as a university lecturer in Germany) about courts,
courtiers and courtly culture in early modern Europe. Because of the Nazi
seizure of state power in Germany early in 1933 this text was to remain
unpublished for more than 35 years. Elias fled first to France and then to
England. He was interned as an enemy alien for about eight months early
in the Second World War, but later became a British citizen. His mother
was killed in Auschwitz. During and after the war he earned a meagre living
by lecturing to adult education classes. With S. H. Foulkes, a friend from
his Frankfurt days, he helped to found Group Analysis, which became
an important school of psychotherapy. Finally, in 1954, he was appointed a
lecturer, and later Reader, in sociology at the University of Leicester. In
1962–4, after his formal retirement, he went to West Africa as Professor of
Sociology at the University of Ghana, a vivid experience for him, in the
course of which he acquired a large collection of African art. From the mid-
1960s, Elias held Visiting Professorships in Germany and the Netherlands.
Between 1978 and 1984 he was a Permanent Fellow-in-Residence at
the Zentrum für Interdisziplinäre Forschung, Bielefeld. He also made
two shorter visits to the USA, giving lectures in New York, Boston, and
Bloomington, Indiana. Leicester remained his main home until 1978, when
he moved to Amsterdam, where he died on 1 August 1990. International
celebrity came to him only towards the end of his long life. In 1977 he was
the first recipient of the prestigious Theodor W. Adorno Prize awarded by
the city of Frankfurt; in 1988 he was the first winner of the Premio Europeo
Amalfi; the Universities of Bielefeld and Strasbourg conferred honorary
doctorates on him; and he was honoured with high national decorations
by both Germany and the Netherlands.

Elias completed his most famous book, *Über den Prozess der Zivilisation*
(now widely known as *The Civilising Process*) during his early years of exile.
It was published by an émigré press in Switzerland in 1939. Attracting
little attention at the time, its greatness was widely recognised only when it
was republished thirty years later. In a poll carried out in 1998 by the
International Sociological Association, it was ranked among the ten most
important sociological works of the twentieth century. Elias took a lively
interest in all aspects of human life, past and present, and continued to
develop the theory of civilising processes in many directions. Throughout
his life, he elaborated a sociological theory of the growth of knowledge
and the sciences. He always sought a secure basis for human knowledge in

order to 'steer between the Scylla of philosophical absolutism and the Charybdis of sociological relativism'. He pioneered the sociological study of sport, and wrote insightfully about art and literature. The common thread was always how people's individual emotions and thoughts are embedded in bonds of social interdependence, and change in accordance with long-term changes in the overall structure of these bonds.

Apart from *The Civilising Process*, all of Elias's 15 books and most of his essays were published after he had formally retired. Some of these works were first written in English, some in German. The Collected Works to be published by UCD Press will include all of his printed works, including many never before available in English.

NOTE ON THE TEXT

This is the first volume of the English edition of the Collected Works of Norbert Elias (1897–1990). It includes all the known texts that Elias published before the appearance in 1939 of his most famous book, known in English as *The Civilising Process*. The sole exception is *The Court Society*, which is based on his 1933 *Habilitation* thesis, and was published at the time only in the technical sense of having been presented to the University of Frankfurt. That will appear, with revisions and corrections, as volume 2. Of the ten pieces collected in this volume, five have not appeared in English before: 'Three-day excursion to the Riesengebirge'; 'On seeing in nature'; 'Idea and individual: a critical investigation of the concept of history' (Elias's doctoral dissertation); 'Idea and individual: a contribution to the philosophy of history' (summary of the dissertation); and 'Anecdotes'.

The Collected Works are intended to provide a definitive English edition of the published works of Elias. His many essays have remained widely dispersed among journals and edited books. In principle the volumes in the series will contain only those texts which Elias actually published, or otherwise authorised for release into the public realm. Some marginal exceptions will be made to this rule, which will be explained by the editors of the relevant volumes. In the present case, the one exception is the inclusion in an appendix of an unpublished document that is of some significance for Elias's later writings. But in general, draft manuscripts, lecture notes, correspondence and similar documents will be excluded. A large archive of these materials exists in the Deutsches Literaturarchiv in Marbach am Neckar, Germany, and can be accessed by scholars for research purposes.

The first two texts in this volume date from the time when Elias was an active member of the Zionist youth movement Blau-Weiss in Breslau (now Wrocław in Poland). This association, and others like it, was modelled on non-Jewish German counterparts. Its members regularly went hiking in the countryside, in so doing communing with nature and simultaneously celebrating both their German and Jewish identities. The 'Excursion to the Riesengebirge' (essay 1) is a short report of Elias's impressions of such a walk in 1914. It was written when Elias was 17 years old and still a student of the Johannes Gymnasium in Breslau. In Elias's later *Reflections on a Life* (1994) he said that at this school he was taught literature and philosophy (particularly Kant) by some very talented teachers, including Julius Stenzel, who later became a Professor at the University of Kiel.[1] He also learned the literature of the ancient Greeks and Romans. That the humanistic and literary part of Elias's education prepared him well for understanding human problems shows even in this short report in his remarks about a family he encountered in a village. One can also sense the emergence of the joyful curiosity about the world so characteristic of the Elias we later knew.

The contrasting second piece, 'On seeing in nature', from 1921 (essay 2) is a full-blown academic article which blends the acute observations of nature of the regular rambler with considerable analytical sophistication, erudition and even precociousness. By the time it was written Elias was working on his doctoral dissertation in philosophy at the University of Breslau. 'On seeing in nature' contains proto-sociological reflections about the link between nature as seen by science and nature perceived as a landscape, which Elias was to develop in later writings. It is also clear from this piece how the two strands of his education – the humanistic-literary and the biological-medical – had been successfully fused. Elias is able to write confidently and with obvious understanding about nature from both the scientific and cultural perspectives. In contrast to many of his contemporaries, right from the beginning Elias's outlook was never narrowly belletristic. Unusually for a social scientist, he was at home in both the social and natural sciences, something which again showed in his later essays and books on the sociology of knowledge and the sciences (to be published in future volumes of the Collected Works).

Elias studied for his doctorate under the neo-Kantian philosopher Richard Hönigswald (1875–1947), who was at that time Professor of

---

1 Stenzel later published a book on the philosophy of language (*Philosophie der Sprache* (Munich: Oldenbourg, 1934)), expressing ideas that may have had some relevance for Elias's thinking, particularly for his application of *Gestalttheorie* to sociology and for what he wrote very much later on language in *The Symbol Theory*. See Helmut Kuzmics's note about this in *Figurations: Newsletter of the Norbert Elias Foundation* 15 (July 2001).

Philosophy at the University of Breslau. In common with other doctoral students of his generation, Elias spent short periods of time at other universities whilst working on his thesis. In the summer semester of 1919 he visited Heidelberg, where he attended the seminar of Heinrich Rickert and also befriended the philosopher Karl Jaspers. In the summer of 1920 Elias went to Freiburg, where he took part in Edmund Husserl's Goethe seminar. Martin Heidegger was also teaching there as Husserl's assistant (a post he held between 1919 and 1923). It is possible that Heidegger and Elias met because Husserl always encouraged his students to attend Heidegger's seminars.[2]

In 1922 Elias submitted his doctoral dissertation, 'Idea and individual: a critical investigation of the concept of history' (essay 3), to Hönigswald. The first 54 pages of the text have been preserved in the Preussische Staatsbibliothek in Berlin. The present translation was made from the version which appears in the *Frühschriften*, the first volume of the German edition of the Complete Works, which was based on the original manu-script. The format of the dissertation conforms to a common pattern of German philosophical theses of the time. It is in the form of an extended rigorous philosophical argument and contains only two sections, no footnotes and no direct quotations from other authors, apart from a long passage from Ernst Cassirer's *Kant's Life and Thought* of 1918.[3] More paragraph breaks have been provided in the English version to make this rather involved text more accessible.

In common with many other younger philosophers at this time, Elias was rebelling against the neo-Kantians' idealism, individualism and neglect of concrete realities. The institutional prominence and mandarin authority of this philosophical establishment were substantial.[4] Elias was part of a wider movement of intellectual opposition in the 1920s (which included the existentialists and fundamental ontologists such as Heidegger) to the rationalism of Kantianism. In that sense, Elias was riding a critical wave not of his own making. But the particular character of Elias's radical approach to a critique of Kant in the dissertation became a serious

2   Richard Wolin, *Heidegger's Children: Hannah Arendt, Karl Löwith, Hans Jonas, and Herbert Marcuse* (Princeton, NJ: Princeton University Press, 2003), p. 216.

3   Ernst Cassirer, *Kants Leben und Lehre* (Berlin: Bruno Cassirer, 1918); trans. James Haden as *Kant's Life and Thought* (New Haven CT: Yale University Press, 1991).

4   Klaus Christian Köhnke, *The Rise of Neo-Kantianism: German Academic Philosophy Between Idealism and Positivism*, trans. R. J. Hollingdale (Cambridge: Cambridge University Press, 1991).

problem for his relationship with Hönigswald. The dispute between them delayed the award of the doctorate. Because of Elias's controversial views about the supposedly timeless status of the a priori and of the principle of *Geltung* (validity), Hönigswald initially refused to accept the dissertation.

In a manner different from many of his German philosophical contemporaries, Elias did not attempt in the thesis to build another philosophy to replace the discredited Kantianism (as the existentialists did, for example). Rather, he embarked on the first steps of his journey towards the total rejection of philosophy itself as an intellectually credible discipline. This was, to say the least, a controversial stance and it was one that was to shape much of his later work and its reception. Even if it is not explicitly stated in the part of the manuscript which has survived, the import of Elias's argument is to cast doubt upon the status and warrant of philosophy itself.

Elias had to make concessions in order to satisfy Hönigswald and to secure the award of the doctorate. This accounts for the obvious contradiction between statements made in the dissertation about the dubiety of epistemological invariants and the complete endorsement of three invariants in the summary of the dissertation, published two years later. This summary forms the shorter text 'Idea and individual: a contribution to the philosophy of history' of 1924 (essay 4). This was the document that was required for the award of a doctorate and went into the formal records.

A version of the dissertation itself was then resubmitted in 1924 and accepted by Hönigswald. On the cover page of the original typescript a note in square brackets in Elias's handwriting says 'pages 55–7 missing', with no further explanation. It is reasonable to speculate that these missing pages contained remarks about various concepts and doctrines – including, possibly, comments on the status of philosophy itself – that were particularly unacceptable to Hönigswald. He would not have wanted them to remain in the dissertation document in the permanent archive of the University and other libraries. The extraction of the last three pages may have been part of the compromise he and Elias reached. Whatever were the true facts of this matter we may never know, but the upshot of this dispute was effectively to end any possibility of Elias making a university career in philosophy at Breslau.

The next text, 'Anecdotes' of 1924 (essay 5), dates from an interruption in Elias's academic career. He had been forced to start work as a salesman of metal pipes for a Breslau metal goods manufacturer in order to support himself and his parents. Their fortune, as well as their income, which consisted of rents on property, had been completely devalued by the German inflation of the early 1920s. Elias wrote 'Anecdotes' on his travels through Europe for this company. The inspiration for the article came from four stories which Elias took from the works mainly of Arrian and Plutarch, but also probably drawing on other sources. Elias uses the four stories to draw morals and human lessons relevant to events of the time. The stories invite reflection – sometimes serious, sometimes whimsical – on honour in victory and in business and upon the brevity of human life. Elias planned to earn money with further publications of this type, but did not get beyond this one, which appeared in the *Berliner Illustrirte Zeitung* (contemporary spelling) in 1924 under the name of Dr Michael Elias. The reason for the different first name has not been established.

With his doctorate in philosophy secure, Elias went to Heidelberg in 1924 as a graduate student, abandoning philosophy and attending the seminars in sociology of Alfred Weber and of the *Privatdozent* Karl Mannheim, with whom he became good friends. He helped to run seminars for him at the Institut für Sozial- und Staatswissenschaften. There Elias began working on his *Habilitation* thesis under Alfred Weber, on the hypothesis that the genesis of modern natural sciences and painting in the Italian Renaissance were both connected to the same fundamental transformation in the mental-spiritual attitude of Western people. (He returned to this theme in a late work, *Involvement and Detachment* of 1987, which will appear as volume 8 of the Collected Works.) A draft outline of the thesis, partly in note form, was discovered among the papers of Alfred Weber in Heidelberg University Library, and it is included here as an appendix because of the significant light it throws on Elias's much later writings on the arts and sciences.

The two contributions to the discussions at the Sixth Conference of German Sociologists held in Zürich in 1928, published in 1929, date from this period. One is a response to a lecture given by Karl Mannheim on 'The importance of competition in the intellectual field' (essay 6). (Mannheim's lecture is more widely known by the title given to it by its English translator, 'Competition as a cultural phenomenon', published in Mannheim's posthumous *Essays in the Sociology of Knowledge*.[5]) Elias's

---

5 Karl Mannheim, *Essays on the Sociology of Knowledge*, ed. Paul Kecskemeti (London: Routledge & Kegan Paul, 1952).

comments show, amongst other things, how his intellectual sympathies had shifted away from Alfred Weber towards Mannheim, whose programmatic theses he welcomes enthusiastically. A slightly abridged translation of Elias's remarks was previously published in 1990.[6] The present translation was made afresh by Edmund Jephcott. An extra paragraph break has been added to make the text more accessible.

In the other response made by Elias at the 1928 conference to a paper by the anthropologist Richard Thurnwald, 'On primitive art' (essay 7), there is an adumbration of one of the underlying motifs of *The Civilising Process* – that in order to understand oneself, it is necessary to go back far into the past. With a few minor corrections, this translation is similar to that included in the Blackwell *Norbert Elias Reader*.[7]

'The sociology of anti-Semitism' (essay 8) appeared in the *Israelitisches Gemeindeblatt*, the official publication of the 'Israelite communities of Mannheim and Ludwigshafen', in December 1929. During the Weimar Republic, the city of Mannheim had the largest Jewish community in the state of Baden, which community published the influential *Israelitisches Gemeindeblatt*. This journal published relatively long articles, such as Elias's piece, whereas the periodical of the Jewish community of Heidelberg, where Elias lived at this time, accepted only family news items. The article shows the early influence of Mannheim on Elias's thinking. But it also shows how, of all members of the Karl Mannheim circle, Elias, at this time still a Zionist, probably had the most developed sociological understanding of the politics of Jewish assimilation and anti-Semitism.[8]

Elias's thesis on the origins of modern science was never completed. In late December 1929 Karl Mannheim was appointed to a chair of sociology at the University of Frankfurt, commencing his duties in the summer semester of 1930. At Mannheim's request, Elias went with him to Frankfurt, as his official Assistant. Elias broke off his *Habilitation* project with Alfred Weber, transferring his supervision to Mannheim and changing the topic of the research. The topic with Mannheim was 'Der höfische Mensch: Ein Beitrag zur Soziologie des Hofes, der höfischen Gesellschaft und des

---

6 Translated by Steven Bucher and Volker Meja, in Volker Meja and Nico Stehr (eds), *Knowledge and Politics: The Sociology of Knowledge Dispute* (London: Routledge, 1990), pp. 97–9.

7 Johan Goudsblom and Stephen Mennell (eds), *The Norbert Elias Reader: A Biographical Selection* (Oxford, Blackwell, 1998), pp. 9–11.

8 With a few minor corrections, this translation is similar to the one by Eric Dunning and Stephen Mennell in the *Journal of Classical Sociology* 1: 2 (2001), pp. 219–25.

absoluten Königtums' (The court person: A contribution to the sociology of the court, court society and the absolute monarchy).

In Frankfurt, the Department of Sociology shared a building with the *Institut für Sozialforschung*, the group of philosophers, economists and Marxists, including Theodor Adorno and Max Horkheimer, who subsequently went into exile in the USA, returned to Germany after the Second World War and later became well known as the Frankfurt School. The two institutions were in fact entirely separate entities; each pursued different kinds of research and relations between them were cordial but distant.[9] Elias himself, however, got on well with Adorno.

One other piece which appears in the German counterpart of this volume, the *Frühschriften*, dates from this time, but has been omitted from this edition. It is 'The clouds or politics as science', a drama sketch with songs adapted from Aristophanes, written by the 'Sociological Collective 1930'. It was performed as a farewell celebration by some of Mannheim's students, including Richard Löwenthal and Boris Goldenberg (who had central roles), when Mannheim left Heidelberg for Frankfurt. Elias participated in this performance. The Editorial Advisory Board for the Collected Works in English was not satisfied that this piece met the criterion of proven authorship by Elias; nor was it authorised for publication in his lifetime.

The coming to power of Hitler in January 1933 put an end to the burgeoning Sociology Department in Frankfurt, as well as to many other university research institutes and art and design schools in Germany, including the Bauhaus. Following the passing of the new law 'for the restoration of civil servants to their offices' in March 1933, which empowered the government to dismiss non-Caucasian state officials (which would include university teachers), a number of Jewish professors and other teachers were dismissed from their posts across Germany. In Frankfurt, these included Mannheim, Theodor Adorno, Max Horkheimer and Adolf Löwe, as well as the non-Jewish, socialist theologian Paul Tillich. All of them, including Mannheim, were forced to leave Germany hurriedly in the months that followed, in order to seek a livelihood as academics elsewhere. Elias was unable to give the public lecture that would have completed the process of *Habilitation* and he, too, was forced to leave. Elias initially visited Switzerland to seek an academic position, but found no

---

9 See Artur Bogner, 'Elias and the Frankfurt School', *Theory, Culture and Society* 4: 2–3 (1987), pp. 249–85.

opportunities, and then moved on to Paris, joining the many German exiles who lived there.

The last two texts date from the two-year period (1933–5) that Elias spent living in the Montparnasse district of Paris, trying to make contact with French academics, including Alexandre Koyré whom he came to know quite well. But with the same result: no jobs were available. He also tried to support himself through an unsuccessful business selling children's toys, but lost all his money. In spite of these setbacks, Elias still managed to continue his research and writing. Each of the two pieces had been carefully tailored by Elias to suit the character of the periodical in which it appeared.

'The kitsch style and the age of kitsch' (essay 9) appeared in January 1935 in the political and literary monthly *Die Sammlung* (The Collection). This was a German exile periodical published by Querido Verlag in Amsterdam and edited by Klaus Mann (1906–49), whom Elias had met by chance in Paris. In his autobiography *The Turning Point* (1984), Mann said that he sought contributors for the periodical from widely international backgrounds.[10] They included a number of celebrities, notably Stephen Spender, Benedetto Croce, Boris Pasternak and André Gide. An integral part of each issue was devoted to anti-Nazi exposures, satires and statistics. Elias's piece does not, however, obviously contain this kind of content. With a few minor corrections, this translation is similar to the one in *The Norbert Elias Reader.*[11]

'The expulsion of the Huguenots from France' (essay 10) dates from the same period and was published in *Der Ausweg: Monatschrift für Umschichtung Wanderung Siedlung* (The Way Out: Monthly Journal for Regrouping, Migration, Settlement), an exile periodical published in Paris. This periodical, which appeared only up to 1935, formed a 'platform for the informed discussion, free of all party politics but convinced of the importance of the colonialist idea, of all questions concerning professional regrouping, migration and settlement'. It also contained practical information on emigration, especially to Palestine, and guidance from the League of Nations Commission for Refugees, as well as conceptual discussions and major articles. The publishing association, Renouveau,

10 Klaus Mann, *The Turning Point: Thirty-Five Years in This Century: The Autobiography of Klaus Mann* (New York: L. B. Fischer, 1942).

11 Goudsblom and Mennell (eds), *The Norbert Elias Reader*, pp. 26–35.

was 'an association for Jewish agricultural interests'.[12] The vivid depiction of the expulsion of the Huguenots contained in Elias's article, particularly the way in which they were socially degraded, excluded from office and expelled from France, has clear contemporary parallels with the similar fate of the German Jews. Typically, though, Elias pulls back from making these parallels explicit. With a few minor corrections, this translation is similar to the one in *The Norbert Elias Reader*.[13]

The main problems of translation in connection with this volume arose in relation to Elias's doctoral dissertation (essay 3) and to a lesser extent its summary (essay 4). The former text, in particular, was written in an involved style typical of the neo-Kantian philosophy of the time and contains a good deal of technical philosophical terminology which represents a challenge for the translator. In consultation with Edmund Jephcott, I made various decisions about certain important words and expressions crucial to the translation, as follows.

Elias makes extensive use in the dissertation of the key Kantian term *Geltung*, which has been translated according to common practice as 'validity'. A related term, *Geltungsgebiet*, meaning large-scale areas of knowledge or perhaps even disciplines, has been translated as 'area of validity'. *Geltungsgemäßheit* became 'validity-adequacy'. Another key pair of terms from the dissertation is *Grund und Folge*, which has been rendered as 'reason and consequence'. These terms are intended to be derived from the language of formal logic and then used to prove that this kind of logic is inadequate for historical judgements. Elias's aim seems to be to turn this logic against itself. Occasionally, however, *Grund* has been translated as 'ground(s)', especially in the plural. Another frequent piece of terminology involves compounds of *Zusammenhang*, especially *Urteilszusammenhang*, which has been translated as 'complex of judgements' for this and similar instances. *Gegenstand* has been rendered as 'object' throughout, except where it specifically means 'subject matter'. The term *das Ich*, which occurs frequently in the dissertation, has been generally translated as 'I' and occasionally as 'self', where 'I' was inappropriate. '*Ich-bezogen*' has been translated as 'ego-related' in preference to 'person-related', which it was felt had a slightly over-modern ring. *Verstand* was translated as 'understanding' and

12 These statements of the objectives of the journal *Ausweg* are quoted from the Editorial Note to the first volume of Elias's Collected Works in German *Frühschriften* (Frankfurt: Suhrkamp, 2002), p. 178.

13 Goudsblom and Mennell (eds), *The Norbert Elias Reader*, pp. 18–25.

Vernunft as 'reason', again following the established convention in translations of German philosophy. The problem of translating *Aufhebung* has been long recognised. The main meanings are abolition, cancellation or suspension. It also has strong Hegelian connotations of abolishing while transcending to a higher level. Elias does not use the word much, but where he does it has been translated as either 'supersession' or 'superseding'. Elsewhere in the volume, *Schicht* was translated as stratum or, in some contexts, groups; and *Ständestaat* as polity of estates.

On the subject of gendered language, it was felt that modernising Elias's 1920s diction using the devices of 'his/her' and 'he/she' would not have been faithful to the linguistic usages and assumptions he and others then followed. The problem was minimised as far as possible by using the plural. The issue is complicated by the fact that Elias often uses the word *Mensch*, which in earlier translations of Elias was sometimes rendered as 'man', when in fact it actually means 'person'. Depending on context, the latter will be the generally favoured translation of the German word in the Collected Works.[14]

In minor respects, editorial practice in the English Collected Works will differ slightly from that of the German editors. Rather than giving detailed editorial notes in a separate appendix, we have decided to insert them as necessary among Elias's own notes. In this volume only two notes are by Elias, in essays 2 and 8; these have been marked 'N.E.' and all other notes have been supplied by me. We have followed our German colleagues in supplying a general bibliography, which shows at a glance all the works that Elias cited or alluded to, as well as those recommended by the editor for understanding the provenance of the texts or as background reading on the period in which these texts were written.

I should like to thank Reinhard Blomert, Johan Goudsblom, Edmund Jephcott, David Kettler, Stephen Mennell, Hugh Ridley, Andrew Smith and Keith Thomas for their advice in the preparation of this volume.

RICHARD KILMINSTER
Leeds, April 2005

---

14   For a sociological discussion of the use of the term 'man', see Johan Goudsblom, *Sociology in the Balance* (Oxford: Blackwell, 1977).

Early Writings

1

Three-day excursion to the Riesengebirge

Day 1   Agnetendorf – Schneegrubenbaude – Elbfallbaude –
Panschefall – Schüsselbauden

Day 2   Spindelmühl – Keilbauden – Rennerbauden – Fuchsberg – Petzer

Day 3   Grenzbauden – Forstbauden – Schmiedeberg

That was our route; anyone who is especially interested should look it up
on a map. I shall note down anything that occurs to me as worthy of
recording. As we climbed from Agnetendorf we noticed that nature is
beautiful even when you can't see it. A dense mist was spread above us, and
higher up it was even snowing. But as we reached the Elbgrund region the
scene below us was like a heaving, billowing sea. Above us the sky was clear
again, and the mist lay far below.

Then we climbed back down into the mist and went striding onwards,
always along the Elbgrund valley. Suddenly, high above, there appeared
three high peaks of reddish rock, a magnificent sight. We stood a long
while gazing. The next morning we were awoken by brilliant sunlight, and
we hurried on in a happy mood through the sunny woods with their sparse
autumn colours. Another image: we are looking for somewhere to stay in
the Christmas holidays. We enter small farmhouses. The children look at
us half shyly, half curiously, and the farmer's wife is a little shy as well. Only
the youngest child is quite unabashed. He is lying on a few old blankets on

Translation of 'Die dreitägige Riesengebirgsfahrt', *Blau-Weiss-Blätter: Mitteilungen des Jüdischen Wanderbundes Blau-Weiss* 1: 11 (Feb. 1914), p. 6.

The Riesengebirge, or 'Giant Mountains', form the border between present-day Poland and the Czech Republic and are known for their ski resorts. The highest peak is Snezka (1602 m.). Elias mentions the region again in essay 2, 'On seeing in nature', pp. 5–21 below.

the floor without a stitch of clothing, cooing merrily at the world in general. As we leave the little house the young people of the village are just coming out of school. Off they hurry, glad like us to be free of constraint. A few of them scuffle, others tease the girls (something we do not do, of course, as well-mannered city folk). There's much more I could tell about what we saw on our outing. You experience much more in three days than in a week here in the city. But my report must be on its way.

Shalom! Norbert Elias, Breslau.

2

On seeing in nature

Indes mich wandernd durch die Weiten
Des Seins Unendlichkeit ergreift,
Indes mein Geist Vergangenheiten
Und Zukunft augenblicks durchschweift

Eint sich das unermessne Viele
Der Schmelzen ungebärd'ger Schwall
Gebändigt zu dem einen Ziele
Aus allen Dingen wird das All.

Da spür ich Leben rings empfahen
Von neuem Atem Feld und Wald
Und alles Ferne will sich nahen
Und alles Nahe nimmt Gestalt.

Das aber ist des Wunders Fülle
Wie Eines sich in Alles zweigt
Aus Rätsels Haft gelöster Hülle
Ein neues Rätsel fruchtbar steigt [1]

[As I wander through wide spaces, overcome by the infinity of being, as my
mind roams in an instant through past and future,

Translation of 'Vom sehen in der Natur', *Blau-Weiss-Blätter: Führerzeitung: Breslauer Heft* 2, 8–10
(1921): 133–44 [*Translator's note*. 'Führer' here refers to youth group leaders.]

1   These stanzas appear to have been written by Elias himself. It was a common practice
amongst scholars of Elias's generation to compose verse or prose in the style of Greek, Roman
and other authors. Elias wrote many poems of various types throughout his life, some of
which were collected in his *Los der Menschen: Gedichte/Nachdichtungen* (Frankfurt am Main:
Suhrkamp, 1988).

The multitudinous vastness, the restless flood of melting things are all
made one, subdued by the single goal; all things become the universe.
Now all around I feel new life, new breath enters field and wood, and all
that's far seeks to draw near and all that's near takes on clear shape.
But most miraculous of all is how one thing merges into all, and how, set
free from the shell of mystery, a new and fruitful mystery arises.]

I

Seeing in nature seems at first the simplest thing in the world. As we walk in
the country we take pleasure in the changing landscape, climb a mountain
and enjoy the beautiful view. And while art may demand the most diligent,
detailed labour if one is to learn to see, nature appears to reveal its beauty
to the eye directly and effortlessly. Despite these differences, a work of
painting has much in common with a natural scene. Both are referred to
not improperly as a 'picture', since in both cases a viewing subject stands
opposed to something to be judged beautiful. But whereas, in the case of
a painting, it can be readily understood why one thing represented – a tree,
a human figure or a building – combines with another to form a painterly
whole, since the artist's imagination has so ordained, it is by no means the
same with landscape. How does it come about that tree and river, meadow
and mountain, road and village likewise complement each other, form a
pictorial unity and – what is still more remarkable – why are there no
absolutely unsightly landscapes, while we must condemn as worthless
countless paintings which lack this unity?

Whereas it is necessary to evaluate carefully the fluctuating artistic
value of paintings, there is no such necessity in the case of landscape, which
seems always unchanging. It is precisely this difference which provides at
least a strong incentive to examine the individual element in a painting, to
determine the authenticity of its particular representation and the way it is
incorporated in the whole. An understanding of the value of a work of art
emerges only gradually from a consideration of the details. In face of a
landscape, by contrast, it is even uncertain where the noteworthy details
actually are. What is it about their particular placement and integration in
the whole that would merit investigation, in the sense that they might teach
us how to see their unity anew and on a deeper level? More and more
bushes, lakes and flowers meet the eye, no doubt of manifold kinds and

nuances, but the bush remains a bush, the flowers are flowers and the lake is a lake. What more could one learn to see in this? And yet all that in its totality, the landscape as such, seems more immediately overwhelming than the work of art.

II

It is taken for granted today that nature is apprehended by those walking in the countryside in terms of its beauty, that is, from an aesthetic viewpoint, as landscape. Yet one is seldom aware that this way of looking emerged only gradually, in the Renaissance age.

It is customary to speak of that period as the age of awakening individuality. By this it is meant that here, for the first time, individual personalities not only played the most important roles but also became aware of themselves in their self-contained uniqueness. This form of consciousness is now accepted without hesitation as the self-evident attitude of human beings as such, while in reality it is only the attitude of the modern age. It was actually this consciousness of the self as sharply cut off within its own fate, standing opposed to every other self and to the whole world, as if separated from them by an abyss, which first converted nature into landscape.[2] A tacit assumption underlying the entire perception of nature as landscape is that the onlooker gazes at something opposite to and beyond himself, which always remains at a measured remoteness from his ego. Only when nature was viewed as a picture facing the human being was it possible to think of reproducing it in a painting, of transferring the three-dimensional natural space to the painted surface and expanding the picture space by means of perspective. From that time, through an inverse interpretation of natural space as picture space, nature was seen as landscape. However, in order to reveal what appears self-evident as merely a peculiarity of the modern age, and to make clear the nature of that peculiarity, it is necessary to give an account of another stage of consciousness, and therefore another stage in the way of seeing nature.

2   This is Elias's first published formulation of what he would later call the *homo clausus* mode of self-experience.

III

Anyone who has gained access to the admirable world of the ancient Greeks must have wondered about the striking fact that these people, who lived in the most intimate association with nature, never actually depicted a landscape, and still less did they possess a word for the unknown concept. But it is equally strange that in this culture, which was rich in strong and distinctive personalities, the concept of personality was unknown.

The many constructions and interpretations of the Greek heritage generally obscure the deeper meaning of the Greek attitude to life, because they leave one thing out of account – that the Hellene could never have become conscious of himself as an absolutely separate entity, sharply distinct from the other. In their consciousness, individuals felt themselves strongly to be, beyond all the differences and contrasts, one with the other and with the world, encompassed by the single and eternal order of the universe. Living within this conception of the cosmos, the Greek was untroubled by the question which afflicts the modern age: here the solitary self, there the alien universe. And *noein, phronein*[3] – thinking itself – was not for them, as it often appears today, a subjective faculty of the individual, but a regularity, an order. This explains why Plato, at the high point of the Greek tradition, did not pose the question of the knowledge of goodness and truth as we are accustomed to do, with the knowing subject on one side and the dimly knowable world on the other. His question was directed at the being of goodness and truth, which is a being in the same way as a person, a number or an idea 'is'.

The Greeks animated tree, mountain and sky with the same living gaze with which they looked upon the Olympic Games. Nature for them was no more a landscape confronting them than the racing youths, the public meetings, the daily bustle of Piraeus or the tragic dramas were merely an overwhelming spectacle. Only if we realise this will the secrets of the Greek attitude to life be revealed to our consciousness. We should never forget that their statues were not carved in order to present a

---

3   The Greek words *noein* (νοεῖν) and *phronein* (φρονεῖν) refer to two types of thinking, respectively 'intelligising' and practical thinking. Elias's argument in the text at this point is that the Greeks of antiquity did not experience their individuality so intensely as people today, which was reflected in the character of their philosophy. For the Greeks, the two words did not express two modes of the *subjective* capacity of an individual facing an alien and unknowable reality as they do today (there is a clear Kantian allusion here). Rather, they expressed the being, or regularity, of the world itself, as a single order.

pleasing spectacle isolated in a museum. Their purpose is fulfilled only when they are set in relation to daily life by particular surroundings, whether as divine images in temples or as ornamentation for streets and houses. For this reason the meaning of Pindar's odes to the victors in the games, for all the splendour of their language and rhythms, remains doubtful and empty to those accustomed to praising victors for their fine appearance or their good bearing, or because they have triumphed in the kind of show which our 'sporting' events usually are, or for the measurably superior performance they have exhibited to the overstretched nerves of the spectators. Pindar, by contrast, praised them because victorious life deserved to be celebrated in song, because the poet on whom a god had bestowed the gift had the happy duty to extol extraordinary life for its own sake, in heaven and on earth. At the same time these songs confirm for us how little importance the Greeks attached to the individual person who had such and such characteristics. They praise the victor for the objective achievement, for the victory, not for his personal merits. They sing his praises from the same point of view, despite all the differences, as Homer sang of the wanderings of Odysseus, of the armour of Achilles, the work of Hephaestus.[4] When the Greeks narrate how Demeter, the earth mother, wanders across the fields in dark garments uttering lamentations, searching by the unsteady light of torches for her daughter abducted by Hades, this is, in its original meaning, neither an image nor a symbol; it is filled with the same life which they themselves lived. In the most mundane ramifications of Hellenic culture we find the same attitude of consciousness from which grew the lofty idea of the cosmos as one world, formed by one order, adorned by one beauty. But to avoid lending new credence to the myth of their eternal serenity, it should also be pointed out that this law held sway over human beings implacably and ineluctably; and the discerning reader may surmise what a mighty power it was that the Greeks called fate. It may be said with good reason, therefore, that this people did not have a Spinozan or a pantheistic religion, as is too often supposed, but lived with nature in an intimate way that is unique and cannot be exhausted by any catchphrase. It should be understood simply as it was, and as is intimated by the breadth of the concept of *physis*.

4   Schiller's essay, 'On naïve and sentimental poetry' provides a particularly valuable and profound supplement on this whole subject (N.E.). [A translation of this essay is to be found in Friedrich von Schiller, *Naïve and Sentimental Poetry, and On the sublime: Two essays*, trans. Julius A. Elias (New York: F. Ungar, 1966) (ed.).]

IV

There is always a danger, in historical investigations, that researchers will either wrongly take themselves and their own world as the basis of the earlier one, or conversely, on encountering something alien and unfamiliar, will prematurely break all bridges with the past and declare all understanding impossible. However, careful appraisal of precisely what is unfamiliar might bring to light much useful material. As far as the ancient Greeks are concerned, a large proportion of even the most conscientious scholars make the mistake of assuming that what is peculiar to us can be found in the Greek world also. They are misled into this by the close connections between European cultural developments and those of the Greeks, which are seen as the most important starting points of their own tradition. Less careful scholars, meanwhile – who like to shock us with mysteries – are more likely to succumb to the second error. But anyone gifted with finer perceptions and armed with well-considered principles will take the middle path, and give an account of the past which elevates it to the present precisely by bringing it before our eyes in all its peculiarity, its strangeness. Anyone who succeeds in understanding the past in this way fills it with new life, while feeling carried along most agreeably. It may not be immediately apparent how this protracted reference to the Greek way of seeing might have advanced our understanding of 'seeing in nature'. For the present it will be enough to point out that anyone who, starting from the concept of landscape as something opposed to us, has formed a vivid idea of the meaning of that other attitude, will at least have set out on the path to a new understanding. It must have become clear that the way in which we see nature is a far from simple matter, since it is intimately bound up with how we see ourselves and the world in general. It is, in short, very closely connected to all that makes up the peculiarity of a culture. It will therefore be necessary to bring the understanding of nature, like the understanding of any other aspect of culture, within the sphere of education.

V

Earlier, the question was left open as to where the noteworthy details of a landscape are actually to be found. It was the special characteristics of these details, and their integration in the whole, that called for an investigation which would reveal their unity at a deeper level. In seeking to understand any totality, we learn first how to see the *individual parts*, in order to grasp the relationships which bind them into an ordered whole. This whole, understood in terms of its internal order, then in turn gives us an ever-deeper conception of the parts. An understanding of nature, too, can be arrived at only in this way.

What one sees first in nature may be a delicate harmony of colours or a romantic grouping which produces the most agreeable surprise. To the city-dweller nature reveals itself primarily through a few beautiful aspects, in which the onlooker can distinguish, and therefore see, something especially striking: a waterfall, bizarre rock formations, a beautiful ruin, or an unfamiliar view from a high mountain. In less conspicuous places, where only trees, bushes, meadows and streams meet the eye, there is actually nothing to be seen by such viewers, as they cannot pick out any-thing distinctive. Somewhat more experienced onlookers, however, are able to see more because they distinguish more: they are delighted by the infinite variegation in which deciduous and coniferous woods, colourful meadows and cornfields, stand out against one another. They are able to take in picturesque details at a glance; they can distinguish and combine in a single image the looming mass of mountains, the mobile, lightly struc-tured clouds beyond them, the lines of a group of trees or of a well-ordered village, the colourful animation of light and shade. In this way such viewers, gazing attentively, will gradually learn to see something where, to the unpractised eye, no landscape is visible at all – in mist, for example, or in snow, where the calm of a uniform grey or white binds together multiplicity, where the whole scene is broken only by lighter or darker lines and the dominant colour draws the eye beyond all organised structures towards the infinite.

It is at this point, where the senses have been trained by the work of art to be overwhelmed only by prominent lines, and awareness of the purely painterly quality of landscape has been developed to the full, that the education which will lead to a true understanding of nature can begin. For if the lines of the groups of trees are related only very generally to mountain masses and clouds, nothing has yet been fundamentally – that is, thoroughly – understood. Only when the very particular and *unique* configuration of these trees has been grasped is it possible to penetrate further, until slowly, through the painterly veil, the individual face of the tree becomes visible. In order to recognise the tree one needs to know how, through the special requirements of its species, it spreads its roots in this particular soil, raises its trunk and shapes its canopy under the given conditions of sunlight and water. The tree is dependent on light and climate, soil and bacteria – in short, on a thousand forces which influence it in accordance with the laws of its species. Where abundant sunlight is lacking, it twists and contorts itself to capture the scanty rays, and where too much light falls steeply it retracts its leaves and twigs so that the light slips past harmlessly, receiving only the frontal light diffused by the atmosphere; or it forms leaves which are able to reflect back the dangerous light of the hot sun, and which appear glossy to us. There are species which thrive only in rich soil and become stunted in sandy ground, and others which bear most fruit in loose, well-drained soil. Yet others, which take on a wretched aspect in the dry avenues of the cities, assume a proud and noble bearing in the moist climate of lakes and well-watered mountains. Only in this way can we understand the broken and misshapen forms of trees caused by the weight of snow in winter, the violent storms and the brevity of the astringent summer in the high mountains, or the krummholz[5] formed in the harsh climate and the meagre soil of the mountain peaks. Only such considerations allow us to distinguish the different faces of the trees. We see isolated conifers which turn the gnarled branches of their loose canopies in all directions and spread their needles as if with indolence, since the sun shines on them abundantly, whereas the conifers in the forest, shading each other, must confine their branch structures to a narrow space. Broad-leaved trees, too, clearly display this difference. Oaks and beeches which, in dense forests, carefully shape the architecture of their shadowed leaves into mosaics to allow each single leaf to enjoy the light, grow a light, broad, continuous canopy when the utilisation of space, light and soil allow. In this way one gradually learns to understand and see how the forms of the firs of the Black Forest, with their dark, deeply curved branches, differ from those of the Riesengebirge;[6] and how the oak and sycamore growing in the slightly marshy soil of the water-

5   Krummholz – technical term for stunted wind-blown trees growing near the tree line on mountains.

6   Elias was almost certainly drawing on his experiences on a three-day trip walking in the Riesengebirge which he had undertaken seven years before (and possibly other trips to the same or similar regions). Some of these experiences are recorded in the first piece in this volume. An impression of the terrain can be gained from Caspar David Friedrich's painting *Riesengebirge* of 1835, which Elias must have known but does not mention, despite its obvious aptness to the subject matter of this article.

meadows along the Oder near Breslau are differently formed from those in woods cultivated by intensive forestry.

VI

Plants growing on the same piece of ground are therefore by no means so randomly scattered and juxtaposed as must appear to someone who merely enjoys the spectacle of the landscape, without understanding the diversity of their forms or their relationships to one another. It will slowly become apparent how the unbroken colourfulness of the meadow, which is without any strident, discordant tones, and the formal unity of the landscape, have their origin in these same laws of juxtaposition, that is, the same sunlight, the same soil, and so on. To see and comprehend the natural world means to learn to understand all these original connections which, first of all in relation to the soil, are defined in broad terms by the relationships between land formation, species of flora and fauna, and climate.

Rock, for example, is at first sight a relatively shapeless, insignificant mass which attracts notice, if at all, only where it shows a striking variation. But we now place it in relationship to its order, its surroundings. As we investigate its internal stratification, its geological structure, and note how wind or ice masses have smoothed its surface here and seeping water has dissolved and crumbled the hard material there, we have a sudden, direct perception of the power which has shaped the mountains and hills, valleys and hollows, where glaciers once lay, storms raged or a sea covered the land. This specific geological structuring now prepares the soil, and therefore the conditions governing the presence of water and bacteria, for colonisation by specific types of flora and fauna. It sets limits to the forest, inserting, for example, at the edge of the mountains, a fringe of rocky terrain with a thin covering of humus on which woodland cannot become established, but only scrub and plants protected by special characteristics which prevent over-rapid evaporation, so that growth is made possible. Interacting everywhere with this structuring from below is the climate, exerting its influence in the opposite direction. Here a broad sphere is opened to the contemplation of nature, which is characterised in the narrower sense by the laws of weather and cloud formation and the effects of sun and rainfall. Beyond such phenomena, however, this sphere which has its place between earth and sky, the stratified realm of the earth's atmospheric mantle, leads on to a consideration of the relationships between earth and the heavens, between solar systems and galaxies.

This realm, in which all things depend on and are related directly or indirectly to each other, helps to make fully clear, and thus to bring closer to fulfilment, the demand made earlier, that we should strive to understand the cosmos by learning to see the details, and by recognising the relationships which connect them into an ordered, unified whole. This whole in turn yields an ever-deeper understanding of the individual detail, which again reflects back on and enlarges the concept of wholeness, of the universe. This unending, to-and-fro process now becomes recognisable as the process by which nature reveals itself to the person who knows, the person who can see.

VII

The path to an understanding of nature is therefore opposed in an important way to the one which leads to the comprehension of a work of art. In the latter, the more mature gaze looks past the subject matter to the manner of its representation – the pictorial form. The contemplation of nature, by contrast, requires the viewer to leave behind the mere enjoyment of pictorial coherence – to leave behind landscape – and to penetrate ever more deeply into the material connections and their laws. In other words, it follows the path of scientific research. Learning to see nature does not mean being passively moved by the subject matter, but actively taking hold of it and seeing it in a way which evaluates according to scientific criteria.

If one has to explain, for example, the relationships between soil, flora and climate, or the motions of the stars, it is hardly enough to fill the gaps in knowledge with a few fine-sounding fables. The goal of the enquiry is the *truth* of these relationships. Science is nothing other than the path – the *methodos*, the method – which leads towards truth. Wherever a properly posed question is encountered in the world, it can only have meaning if a proper answer – that is an answer which has the purpose of pursuing truth – is possible. Such an answer may not be possible in the present, when the subject matter of the question may be still shrouded in mystery, but it must be possible in principle. And where such an answer is possible, there also is a scientific field. But only someone who by diligent study has become familiar with the foundations of science and its cumulative results – that is, with the course of science – will be qualified to answer the question. Those without learning are fond of asking many questions. It is the task of the educator not only to answer the questions but, above all, to stimulate the questioner with further questions – that is, to point out doubtful areas and correct wrongly posed questions with counter-questions. To answer the question: 'Why do leaves fall in autumn?' by saying: 'Because they grow old' achieves nothing at all. The necessity for leaves to fall can only be demonstrated by showing though observation that only the leaves of trees actually fall, whereas grasses generally wither on the stem, and by gradually introducing the questioner to the methods of botany and plant biology. It will be shown that at the start of the cold season, as light and water grow scarce, the tree withdraws the nourishing sap from the leaves and plugs the ends of the twigs with cork, so that the leaves can fall without damaging the organism, whereas grasses behave differently, in accordance with their different conditions of growth and their different functions. Similarly, the question: 'Why does the sun go down in the evening?' cannot be answered in a few words. To learn to see nature therefore means nothing other than to recognise areas which raise questions, and to evaluate or solve the questions with the theory of the relevant science. This process leads from the questionable nature of a certain subject, through its relation to a scientific theory, to the concept – that is, to the conceptual understanding of the subject – in order first to ground the theory more firmly and extend it on the basis of this understanding, and then to derive new questions from the extended theory. This endless interplay between questions and solutions – solutions in the sense of a theory from which a new question and not just an extended solution emerges – is what we call science, and we do so because, in this unending process, truth is revealed.

The relationship between science and education therefore demonstrates a fundamental principle of all pedagogy: wherever education takes place, questions are asked. They may be questions as to what granite is, or what 'lying' is. For ethical questions are always, and quite wrongly, separated from other scientific questions. A person who distorts truth for the sake of personal advantage, in order to appear superior or in the right, may be called untruthful and a liar. But the meaning of those terms cannot be made clear until it has been repeatedly shown that only scientifically founded answers – that is, answers which lay claim to truth – have any meaning at all. Only such thorough, judicious, scientific educational work makes it possible to pass beyond shallow chatter and vain, boastful duplicity and attain the factual, deep and penetrating clarity which may not be the ultimate goal of all teaching, all education, but must undoubtedly be one of its essential goals. Only painstakingly acquired competence, and an assurance which surveys the whole picture, can impart the attitude which is able to admit to error because it need not be vain enough to deny it, and because its aim is not to secure some faltering personal dignity, but to attain truth. It is therefore only a consciousness of one's own objective achievement that can put an end to the all-too-frequent games of intellectual superiority, and give one the desired assurance.

VIII

The viewpoint now reached may be enough to show that principles of education as a whole are involved in teaching people how to see nature! From this viewpoint, too, a number of ideas introduced earlier, that may have seemed an unnecessary digression at the time, will be more readily understood: the reference to the Greeks.

Anyone who has learned to evaluate and perceive natural processes and relationships in the way described above will long since have bridged the gulf between self and world in a higher sphere, and this viewpoint will be further strengthened by recognising among the Greeks an attitude which, though in many respects different, is the same in its conception of a single, all-embracing order.

It also becomes clear at this point, however, in what respects we have advanced beyond the Greeks. Whereas the Greek cosmos was imbued with a wholly divine order, we, in constantly ascending from new particulars to new distinctions and connections in accordance with the ramification and differentiation of scientific methods, organise and order many hundred times more material than they did. If one enquires into the properties of stone simply as a quantitatively determined mass, e.g. with reference to gravity, the answer will be based on physical theory. If one asks about its material composition, it will be classified according to chemical theories, along with acids, bases, alcohols and fats. If one asks about its age, or the meaning of its stratification, geological theory must provide the answer. And just as the countless interactions between question and answer on the level of theory are organised by different types of scientific methods clearly distinguished from one another, these methods – as is shown by the above example from physics, chemistry and geology – are nevertheless more or less closely related, despite their clear demarcations. They are united as links in the system of the sciences or – which amounts the same thing – in the idea of science which is fundamental to them all. It can therefore be understood that, as an area of validity of a specific kind, they are distinct from other areas of validity, such as art, religion and law. The totality of these areas – which are all valid in their particular way – the system they form, is the idea of the universe, the cosmos. It is the totality which, as argued above, one has to learn to see all its details in order to recognise the connections which bind it into an ordered whole. In what has been said up to now I have tried to make clear how the perception of the whole enhances the apprehension of the details, and how the deepened relationships between the details in turn enrich and broaden the concept, and therefore the perception, of the whole. If I have succeeded in this, and in bringing clearly into consciousness the unending process by which existence discloses itself to us, I have also made visible the way in which we have surpassed the Greeks. The cosmos of the Greeks is a finite entity resting statically within itself. To the great Parmenides,[7] true being presented itself as a finitely limited globe which existed in motionless repose (and which, for him, was certainly not an image). For us, on the other hand, the ordered world can be visualised as a sphere with a periphery which grows from a centre ever more richly and all-embracingly towards infinity. The content of this order can be understood only if we are aware that order is not a rigid, restrictive skeleton on which to construct the world, but something which makes possible unlimited relationships and perspectives in all directions. In a continuous process it forms being ever anew, while the surface of the sphere arches higher and higher. Only in this way can the purpose of educational work founded on the sciences be understood. The sciences, advancing endlessly by virtue of their very concept, on all sides enlarge our view of an order which is articulated into infinity. In this way, by carefully weighing sameness against difference, the reference to the Greeks may be fruitful for us, and at the same time we may give thanks to Plato,

7   Parmenides, Greek philosopher who flourished in the first half of the fifth century BC. Known for his view that the reality of the physical world is timeless and unchanging, the perception of change being an illusion. This conception contrasted with Heraclitus' view that only movement and flux are real, stability being illusory. It is clear from the text at this point and from many other places in his writings, that Elias's sympathies were always with Heraclitus.

their greatest thinker, to whose inexhaustible influence we owe this way of thinking.

IX

In the foregoing, the example of nature as subject matter for education has been used to illustrate the principles of education as such. Apart from Plato, two men, whose life and work formed more or less explicitly the starting point of this educational tradition, have pointed the way in this discussion: Kant and Goethe. They are mentioned here not only because of the reverence due to them but also because of the nature of our subject. It would serve little purpose to speak at length of Kant here. For those familiar with the complex of ideas making up the transcendental method, the intellectual order evoked by a mention of his work will deepen their understanding of what has been said here, especially as regards the concepts of idea, law, contemplation and science, and the relations between them. To speak of him here for others would be to build on air.

However, all those who claim to be bearers and mediators of cultural values, and therefore all educators, can justly be expected to be familiar with the work of Goethe and the meaning of his life. A few observations will therefore be made on his reflections on nature, as a practical paradigm of what has been argued above.

Almost every artist and, more generally, at least every cultural epoch of the modern era, have selected a particular landscape from the plenitude of the natural world and represented it with especial frequency and love. This was done because that landscape corresponded most closely to a particular cultural disposition. One may recall, for example, the classical landscape of Hölderlin's 'The Archipelago',[8] the romantic scenery evoked by Goethe's *Werther*,[9] or the 'naturalistic' landscape – to touch on this paradox in passing – elaborated by Flaubert.[10] Goethe, by contrast – once he had left Romanticism behind – never again depicted a landscape in the

8 'Der Archipelagus', a poem by the German poet, Friedrich Hölderlin (1770–1843) in which he hoped that modern Germany would become like ancient Greece. The German text and an English translation by Michael Hamburger can be found in Hölderlin, *Poems and Fragments* (Cambridge: Cambridge University Press, 1980), pp. 212–31.

9 Johann Wolfgang von Goethe (1749–1832), *Die Leiden des jungen Werthers* (Leipzig: Weygand, 1774); trans. Michael Hulse as *The Sorrows of Young Werther* (London: Penguin, 1989).

10 Gustave Flaubert (1821–80), French novelist, best known for *Madame Bovary* (1857).

proper, purely pictorial sense of the word. Rather, his intellectual temper, which harks back to ancient Greece far more even than that of the classicist Winckelmann,[11] sought through quiet study in conjunction with science to demonstrate regular relationships through his own contemplative observations, and thus to grasp through the particular the idea contained in the totality. As his lofty standards became ever more perfect in the works of his maturity, the *Italian Journey* and *Wilhelm Meister*,[12] he judged nature with the same impartiality as he judged all human phenomena, and in relation to those phenomena. But the intellectual freedom with which he applied such standards, the clear, Grecian sense of visual form with which he nurtured his theory and developed it through experience – this candid, plastically lucid manner of seeing is the most wonderful attainment of his personality.

The life of Goethe, despite the errors conditioned by his time, demonstrates one thing above all else: that someone who sees the world indistinctly, through a mist of obscure feelings, must necessarily have dull and empty inner experience. But the more diversely the outer world is articulated, the more varied and differentiated existence appears in its order, the richer and more animated becomes the 'inner' life. And as outer and inner intensify each other in a constant interchange, it again becomes apparent why a self which feels divided from the world by an abyss and, engrossed by the murmur of dull feelings, closes its eyes to the richness of the outer world, remains arid, impoverished and empty. An education which fails to transcend this division – a division which finally underlies any vision of nature merely in terms of landscape – therefore remains hollow and poor in content. Only if education draws to itself the whole mass of the world's subject matter and makes use, in its own way and according to its own principles, of the forms in which that subject matter is constantly ordered and re-ordered by the ever-advancing sciences, does it fulfil its educational task. In face of such abundance any lack of subject matter remains incomprehensible.

---

11 Johann Joachim Winckelmann (1717–68), German archaeologist, known for his influential writings on Greek and Roman painting, sculpture and architecture.

12 Goethe, *Italienische Reise* (Leipzig, 1816–17); trans. W. H. Auden and Elizabeth Mayer as *Italian Journey* (London: Collins, 1962). Goethe wrote a series of Wilhelm Meister novels, *Wilhelm Meisters Lehrjahre* (1795–6) and *Wilhelm Meisters Wanderjahre* (1829), trans. R. O. Moon as *Wilhelm Meister: Apprenticeship and Travels* (London: G. T. Foulis, 1947).

X

However, all education by another person, even when its purpose is perceived with utmost clarity, harbours an ultimate danger which cannot be overestimated. Those who in their youth have been influenced by a number of educators may easily become so accustomed to enjoying the support of others, and to handing over to them the responsibility for their own actions, that they finally shrink from the effort of acting decisively from their own resources. Where they are forced to act with responsibility they evade the decision with the most wretched irresolution, or fall into the hands of any educator or influence, bad or good, who happens to come along. The further it advances, therefore, education must urge its pupils more and more strictly and deliberately to take responsibility for their own deeds and misdeeds. It teaches them to distinguish between good and evil, beauty and ugliness, truth and falsehood. But these standards remain wooden and useless if those equipped with them are not able to test and prove them again and again through their own experience and reflections, on the basis of their own insight and with responsibility to themselves, and if, as they constantly educate themselves, these standards are not enlarged. All that has been said up to now therefore points compellingly to the following idea as its culmination: that it is the obligation of everyone to form themselves, that is, to educate themselves in awareness of their own responsibility, and that they are for themselves an endless task. To foster the understanding of individuals to the point where they can clearly judge their own possibilities and then judiciously attract to themselves what is beneficial and reject what is harmful, and can take full responsibility for so doing in their own eyes, by the standards of their own understanding of good and evil, true and false – that is the purpose of the education of one person by another. In the end, however, everyone must take charge of his own 'formation'. In this way the idea expressed here is linked at its highest point to the tradition of the eighteenth century. The educational ideal of Goethe's era rises at this point to new significance, far removed from the shallow concept of our time. The formation of a human being is not a formation in the sense in which a snail's shell or a cloud is formed. It is not of the same nature as the shaping of the work of art by the hand of the artist. Rather, human beings, in a wholly incomparable way, take on form under their own hands and through their own understanding. The only way in which they can become fruitful in passing through the particular to the totality of the world is, therefore, by the process described above, in which the sphere arching towards infinity constantly expands its own scope while the inner lives of human beings, in awareness of this entire world, guide themselves to ever richer vision and insight; it is the process of educating human beings. It is clear, therefore, that any standstill, any limitation or postulation of a final state, would mean the cessation of this process of human formation. Having understood this, one can perhaps more readily accept the idea that no historically conditioned ideal image, no final purpose, which could never bring more than a small segment of the infinite cosmos within its scope, could satisfy the pedagogical intention. Only the human being who becomes aware of himself with full responsibility as an infinite task fulfils the principles of education. The pre-eminent example of how this task can be taken up with greatest vigour is again provided by Goethe. He, more than any other, was accustomed to surveying his own path in terms of the same clear standards with which he judged the world, doing what was beneficial and dismissing with a calm gesture whatever was harmful. In this way, striding from peak to peak, he formed himself with ever-increasing maturity, and as he surveyed the universe and himself in a single consciousness, the two converged. The Greek cosmos, which embraced the self, the other and the world in an eternal order, was recreated on a new level. In this way the formation of Goethe as a human being, in which the cosmos constantly revealed itself to him with greater abundance and from new directions, ended only with his life. And young generations, building on his creation, now develop the world and themselves in an endless process. But how one generation, from its lofty position, can point the way upwards to the one which follows, is revealed to the gaze which has gained an overview by the image of education:

> *lampadia echontes diadôsousin allêlois.*[13]
> [passing the torch from hand to hand]

---

13 λαμπάδια ἔχοντες διαδώσουσιν ἀλλήλοις This quotation is from Plato's *Republic*, Book I, section 328a (see Plato, *Republic*, trans. Paul Shorey (Cambridge MA: Harvard University Press, 1930), pp. 4–7). Elias used the same image in several other places in his writings on the sociology of knowledge and science to convey the intergenerational process of the creation and transmission of knowledge.

3

Idea and individual: a critical investigation of the concept of history

I

If one tries to form a clear picture of the task of the historical researcher, one arrives at something like the following result: before him lies as it were the material, waiting to be worked on by him – the immense abundance of all that human beings have achieved. Well-considered principles must teach him how to sift this material, selecting what merits his work and leaving aside what is without significance. For this purpose, however, he cannot rely on just any arbitrarily posited precepts; the material itself must contain the conditions which make a selection possible. Only then can he be sure that such a process of sifting is more than a technical and fundamentally inadequate tool of human understanding. The object of historical investigation is not a structureless mass of events which it would be futile to attempt to grasp in retrospect, but a sequence of facts which are organised and linked together by the framework of a characteristic order.

Even if the investigator sets out to understand the object in its incomparable individuality, the more successful he is in singling out this and only this object from the wealth of material, and the more clearly he appears to isolate it from everything that ever was or will be, the more closely will he actually link it to everything else, and the more graphically will the sequence in which the object has its particular place emerge. By the determination of a single fact, other facts in its field which are close to it in time – whether in the field of art, law, science or religion – are at once thrown into sharper relief. The whole of this field, as distinct from any other, will appear in a different light. Finally, the clarification of that

Translation of Norbert Elias's DrPhil thesis, 'Idee und Individuum: Eine kritische Untersuchung zum Begriff der Geschichte', submitted to the Philosophy Faculty of the Friedrich-Wilhelms University, Breslau, July 1922.

individual circumstance places the whole epoch to which it belongs in the new perspective, as a unity which embraces all the individual fields. On the other hand, anyone who views the single fact from the aspect of this unity will no longer perceive it as a seemingly isolated formation, but will learn to understand it in a new sense as a constituent part of its era, contingent on the unique character of that era. This entire, articulated structure, which directs the attention of the researcher from the particular to the whole and then back to the particular, reflects more than a chance point of view – it reflects a particular order of history.

Even a historian who approaches his material with dogmatic prejudices about the laws of history will – if he immerses himself with complete honesty in his subject matter – always be led back to the one method which is imposed by the order underlying the material itself. The more distinctly he perceives the meaning of an individual historical circumstance, the more clearly will his research reveal to him the concepts which people at the time of that circumstance had of God or truth, of morality or beauty – in short, the ideas of that time. And he will learn to understand a specific system of such ideas as the fundamental condition of that time. However, the more he becomes aware of the conditioning unity of the idea in the diversity of manifestations characteristic of one and the same era, the deeper will become his understanding of each individual element of the time, each individual fact, since his understanding is now flooded with relationships deriving from the fundamental unity. But that is not all. As the peculiarity of an individual segment of history gradually emerges more and more clearly from the totality of all others under the historian's gaze, the totality in turn takes on new clarity through the special characteristics which distinguish it from the individual segment. This means that the time-determined forms of the idea themselves combine, as 'individual facts', to form the totality of a system of ideas, and that this system holds together the edifice of history like a scaffold, and organises it as a unity. It is this system, therefore, which provides the point of view, called for above, by which to select what is historically significant.

Now, to make this selection it is important, above all, that the historian should know what is to be understood by an 'idea'. This term, which has been bandied about too much in the course of history, has become so misunderstood that even its cautious use in the preceding discussion can signify nothing more than that there is, underlying history, a peculiar formation which is commonly called an 'idea'. This idea and its relationship to the individual historical fact, to the 'individual' in the widest sense of the term, harbour a particular problem. From the solution to this problem historians may expect to gain clarity on the principle of historical selection and on the legitimacy of their own procedure, while philosophers may hope to gain insight into the structure of history and proof of the claim to truth which historical judgements require.

History and philosophy come together, therefore, in their common interest in the idea. Such convergence between two different disciplines, each of which initially has its own, well-characterised field of study, is one of the problems posed by the concept of the idea. At this point a question of no small importance begins to be posed. If this concurrence between philosophy and history proves well founded, nothing more or less will be demanded than that the critical method of philosophy, with which it grants or denies to the fundamental conditions of an object the right to constitute a principle, must under certain circumstances be placed in the service of historical research. Although detailed reflection may still be needed to investigate this question, one thing can already be stated here: historical research can make no graver error than to act in contravention of the critical method just described. It would do so by applying dogmatically – that is, without testing the legitimacy of its procedure – very particular ideas, which it claims to derive from a few individual facts, to the whole course of history, and by seeking to interpret all the other facts accordingly. To treat the idea in this way as the general law for a multiplicity of individual facts, which are seen as particular cases of that idea, would be to transfer the method of the natural sciences to the discipline of history. The former, in keeping with the peculiar structure of their object, have a right to regard a law derived from analysis of a single case as valid for an infinite multiplicity of particular cases. The method of the natural sciences is therefore characterised by a type of conclusion peculiar to it alone, in which the general law represents the major premise, the particular case the minor premise and the case understood in terms of its general condition, forms the *conclusio*.[1] But whether the method of historical research moves along analogous paths may be regarded from the outset as extremely doubtful.

As is apparent, such ideas touch on highly topical questions of modern historical research. The more clearly this discipline sees its task as

---

1   The word *conclusio*, used here and elsewhere in this text, comes from classical rhetoric and is not synonymous with the English word conclusion. Rather, it means a summation, an argument based on probable premises, as distinct from a demonstration.

that of understanding not only the individual fact but, above all, historical connections, the more urgent becomes the question as to the nature of these connections. Are individual historical facts connected together like particular cases subsumed under the idea as their general condition, or is the conditioning relationship expressed by the concepts of 'idea and individual' actually not identical to the relationship of 'general and particular'? Is it permissible to understand the concepts of, for example, a particular religious or national idea, by analogy with a natural law, as a formula defined by factual content according to which, quite generally, all the individual facts from the history of this religion or this nation can be brought together and determined? Or is the structure of the conditioning unity which, for example, connects together everything which is 'French' and distinguishes it as specifically 'French' from that which is 'German' or 'Russian', a different structure to that of a natural law? These are all questions with which the historian has constantly to contend. However he may decide them, one thing emerges from the questions themselves: historical research will stray from the safe path of method as long as it approaches its object with certain general pre-judgements, and without having tested the legitimacy of its standards. In other words, dogmatic historiography must be replaced by critical[2] historiography.

For periods which seek the truth of an object solely in the form of the 'general', and which expect the general currency of knowledge to spring from its generality, historical research has coined the term 'Enlightenment'. It is immaterial here whether one is entitled to believe that the whole ideas-content of the Enlightenment is exhausted by this notion. It does, at any rate, express one of the core ideas of all Enlightenment philosophy. Be that as it may, it is Enlightenment motifs in the genuine sense of the term which gain predominance in the dogmatic form of historical research, and they lead more or less explicitly to all the consequences which are typical of ages of enlightenment and of their way of viewing history.

Whether the whole of history is seen dogmatically from the point of view of progress, which finally leads humanity to knowledge of universal truth and thus makes such knowledge a universal value by which history is measured; whether religion and everything within history which is understandable only in terms of religion is disdainfully redefined as the religion of reason – the core of which is formed by the general moral law – as

2 The word critical here and elsewhere in the dissertation is being used in its Kantian meaning, rather than the Hegelian one associated with latter-day critical theory.

'religion based on pure knowledge'; whether the nation is replaced by a pallid concept of humanity which at bottom is nothing more than a nebulous generality standing for the multiplicity of human beings; or whether, finally, specific general formulae are invented for each religion and each nation to represent the unity in the diversity of all their manifestations – the method by which a knowledge of history is supposedly achieved is in every case the same: dogmatic or enlightened, as one prefers.

The great discovery of the Enlightenment was that the understanding can autonomously gain knowledge of an object, and for the sake of this discovery it has proudly defended the legitimacy of its understanding against dogmas which could not be founded as knowledge. In relation to the knowledge of history, however, this discovery is now leading enlightenment itself into dogmatism, since it regards the method of gaining knowledge of nature, even if that method is misunderstood, as the method of gaining knowledge as such.

Now that it has been made clear by the example of the Enlightenment what is to be understood by dogmatic historiography, critical historiography requires us to proceed to investigate the concept of the idea. However, one cannot undertake to investigate this concept without having briefly discussed its history. For if a problem, and the concept which is to provide an answer to it, have once taken on in history a formulation as specific as that of the idea and the problem underlying it, both problem and concept can be unambiguously explored only on the basis of that historical formulation.

It was *Kant*[3] who, in responding to a very specific problem – the problem with which he opened the way beyond Enlightenment philosophy – used the concept of the idea. The problem with which the eighteenth-century Enlightenment contended, giving it now a shallower, now a deeper formulation, was the problem of the knowledge of nature. Kant supplied the answer through the deduction of the categories. By making clear the constitutive conditions of the object of experience as conditions of the knowledge of the object, as functions of judgement, he demonstrated the non-empirical, logical character of those conditions. He therefore established the validity of the natural law by defining it as the determination of a system of forms of relationship which were to be demonstrated by analysis of the object of experience, forms which were the conditions of a multiplicity of such objects and in that sense were universal – the categories.

3 Author's emphasis.

But the question touched on above, concerning the conditioning relationship of the kind justified here, led beyond the problem dealt with by Kant. Did that type of relationship, in which the universal law was the condition and the multiplicity of particular cases the conditioned, relate to the object as such, or only to the natural object? Natural laws are no less certain and objectively valid than the object of experience. Being themselves the conditions of an object, they must necessarily be subject in their turn to conditions which are also conditioned. Only the totality of conditions is unconditioned, and this absolute, i.e. no longer conditioned, totality of the conditions of an object is what, for *Kant*,[4] laid claim to the Platonic term of the idea. The question now, however, is how the individual conditions relate to each other. Does each condition stand to what it conditions in the same relationship as the law to the object of experience? In other words, does the series of conditions ascend to a more and more comprehensive universality, until it finally culminates in the idea as the most comprehensive and universal law? It is not possible to say that the Kantian conception of the idea absolutely affirmed the notion of its universality, or that it completely precluded it.

What is certain is that, through the manner of its derivation, it contains, at the least, motifs which, taken to their conclusions, would signify the universality of the idea. For the Kantian idea is derived from the above-mentioned form of conclusion which is characteristic of the natural sciences, a form of conclusion which takes a universal law as the major premise and the particular case as the minor premise, in order to combine law and individual case as the concept of that case in the *conclusio*. If it could be demonstrated that the major premise of this conclusion takes on certainty and objective value as the *conclusio* of such an, as it were, higher conclusion, the major premise of which would therefore be a more universal law, and that all individual conditions are bound together by the same process of deduction, the idea itself would indeed be nothing other than the major premise of such a conclusion; that is to say, it would be the universal law which subsumes under it the totality of the other conditions as particular cases. And anyone who related the idea to individual facts in the manner of a universal law would first have to prove that the connection between the 'particulars' is of the kind just described. As we shall see, however, this proof cannot be furnished. Suffice it to point out here that it is hardly sensible to speak of more universal and most universal laws.

4 Author's emphasis.

Kant himself, in his third *Critique*,[5] found a formulation for the problem underlying the notion of the idea which was destined to cleanse this notion of any suspicion of universality. It does not greatly matter that in that work he did not pose the problem explicitly in terms of the idea, or that he did not elaborate it by the example of the connection between branches of science within the totality of science, but by the example of the objects of biology and of art. Perhaps it was the very tendency towards universality inherent in his notion of the idea which deterred him from such direct elaboration. Perhaps the problem presented itself to him in its full acuity through the examples of the work of art and of the organism just because these entities resisted more strongly any attempt to reinterpret their totality as a generality in relation to particular elements of classification. However that may be, the question that Kant answered in the first two *Critiques*[6] with the notion of the idea receives its most mature and trenchant formulation in the *Critique of Judgement*.[7] And, as is always the case, the historical investigation of a problem turns out here to be fruitful for systematic thought in general. For the gradually advancing severance of the idea from motifs of universality, which was brought to a relative conclusion in the *Critique of Judgement*, is also the task of the modern philosophy of history, if it seeks to establish a critical science of history. A study of the development of the Kantian problem of the idea would therefore directly benefit the work of systematic philosophy.

For reasons which will be apparent shortly, an example given by Cassirer will help to clarify the task with which the *Critique of Judgement* is concerned. Cassirer writes as follows:

> The concrete structure of empirical science confronts us with a peculiar task . . . For here we find not only a lawfulness of events as such, but a connection and interpretation of particular laws of such a type that the whole of a determinate complex of appearances is progressively combined and dissected for our thought in a fixed sequence, in a progression from the simple to the complex, from the easier to the more difficult. If we consider the classical example of

5 Immanuel Kant, *Critique of Judgement* of 1790, trans. Werner S. Pluhar (Indianapolis: Hackett, 1987). It is widely referred to as Kant's Third Critique.

6 Kant's first two *Critiques* were *The Critique of Pure Reason* of 1781, trans. and ed. Paul Guyer and Allen W. Wood (Cambridge: Cambridge University Press, 1998); and *The Critique of Practical Reason* of 1788, trans. Lewis White Beck (Indianapolis: Liberal Arts Press, 1956).

7 Kant, *Critique of Judgement*.

modern mechanics, it is shown in the *Critique of Pure Reason* and in the
Metaphysical Foundations of Natural Science that three general laws of
the understanding correspond to and underlie the three basic laws
laid down by Newton: the law of inertia, the law of the proportionality
of cause and effect, and the law of the equality of action and reaction.
But the structure and the historical development of mechanics is not
thereby adequately circumscribed and comprehended. If we trace
its progress from Galileo to Descartes and Kepler, from these men
to Huygens and Newton, yet another connection than the one stipu-
lated by the three analogies of experience is revealed. Galileo begins
with observations of the free fall of bodies and motion on an inclined
plane, as well as the determination of the parabolic trajectory of a
projectile; Kepler adds empirical determinations of the orbit of Mars,
Huygens the laws of centrifugal motion and the oscillations of a
pendulum; finally all these particular moments are combined by
Newton and are demonstrated to be capable, as thus integrated, of
encompassing the whole system of the universe. Thus in a steady
advance from minor, relatively simple primary elements the entire
picture of the actual is sketched. We reach in this way not just any old
order of events, but an order that our understanding can survey and
comprehend. Such comprehensibility cannot be demonstrated and
seen as a priori necessary through the pure laws of the understanding
alone, however. According to these laws, it could be thought that
empirical reality indeed obeyed the general premise of causality, but
that the various causal sequences which interpenetrate to form it
ultimately determine in it a complexity such that it would be impossible for us to isolate and trace out individually the individual threads
in the whole sprawling tangle of the actual.[8]

The question dealt with by the *Critique of Judgement* can therefore be
summarised as follows: what is the principle by which a multiplicity of
individual entities, for example, individual natural laws, are combined into
a whole, for example, the natural sciences, in such a way that an order
which is 'purposive' for the understanding comes into being? It becomes
apparent straight away that fundamentally the same question is being posed
here as was sketched above in relation to concepts such as a 'religion' and

8   Quoted from Ernst Cassirer, *Kants Leben und Lehre* (Berlin: Bruno Cassirer, 1918); trans.
James Haden as *Kant's Life and Thought* (New Haven CT: Yale University Press, 1991), pp. 291–2.

'nation'. One might, of course, counter Cassirer's example by arguing that Kant was investigating the work of art and the organism. And there is no doubt that the selection of different objects for investigation cannot finally be immaterial to the meaning of the question. But the possibility of seam-lessly developing the core elements of the problem of judgement, the concepts of 'wholeness' and 'purposiveness', by using the example of his-tory proves that this problem is still situated above the level of investigation at which the various 'examples' must necessarily lead to different problems. At the same time, the example of history will show how directly the *Critique of Judgement* continues to develop the problem of the idea from the other two *Critiques*. For the task which science has sought to perform in the course of its history is to understand the object of its investigation from the totality of its conditions. To go beyond the partial condition of the object, as embodied for the natural sciences in the individual law, and to deter-mine the totality of individual conditions – that is the goal of science and the idea of truth, or, which amounts of the same thing, the idea of 'science'.

We earlier rejected the idea that the type of deduction by which the general law of the major premise is connected to the individual case in the *conclusio* can be regarded as the form of the relationship between the individual conditions. What has to be investigated now, therefore, is what the form of this relationship actually is. Such a sequence of ideas brings to light with full clarity and free of obstructions the question central to an investigation which is directed at determining the concept of the idea. The unity of all the individual facts which form part of the history of German art or the history of natural science, for example, is expressed by the concept of the idea. The idea must therefore represent a specific order in the connection of individual objects which are themselves, as functions of the idea, of a specific kind. This, therefore, is an order by virtue of which it is possible to form in relation to such objects judgements which lay claim to truth, that is to say, scientific judgements. And conversely, the relationship by which individual historical facts are connected together can serve as the starting point for an investigation of this order.

It sometimes happens that historical research finds itself suddenly confronted by a phenomenon which is so unique and so seemingly unconnected to the other facts of its time that initially no one is able to explain how it was 'possible', i.e. what were the conditions under which it could come into being. In just this way the science which concerns itself with the history of art found itself confronted at the beginning of this century with the 'riddle of the van Eyck brothers'. Art historians noted with astonishment that these artists had, between 1400 and 1440, produced paintings which seemed entirely unconnected to other works of Gothic painting. In earlier periods of historical research they might well have been satisfied with pointing to the mysterious genius of the great artist as the explanation for such an achievement. However, to determine the individual greatness of the work, and then the unique personality of its creator, by something more than generalities, it was necessary to understand the factual context, i.e. the art-historical context, from which the work emerged in this form and no other. For, to understand a work, to determine the concept of a work or a historical fact, means finding precisely the aspects which made it necessary for the work to be created in this way and not otherwise. Each brushstroke of a painting must, in a sense, be traceable back to causes which themselves follow from causes, which in turn have their causes. Historians therefore seek in paintings on which the artist was schooled causes which played a part in shaping his works, in order to understand how, on the basis of his own character, he evaluated and developed what he had learned, and thus to gain an understanding of his artistic personality. Historical research itself is only possible on condition of such a complex of reasons. The historian assumes that the 'riddle of the van Eyck brothers' can be solved and that the chain of causes leading from the paintings of these masters to other paintings has no missing links. His task is precisely to discover the connection between the individual works.

It is obvious at once that such a complex of reasons connecting individual facts exists not only in the history of art but also in history as such. The single historical fact is always a function of a judgement which has been derived as a consequence from other grounding judgements. The facts of a battle, of a religious foundation, of a legal judgement, and not least the discovery of a natural law – all these can be recognised because a complex system of reasons, and therefore of judgements, has led up to them and determined the course they have taken. The concept of an historical fact can be understood to the extent that the complex of judgements from which it is derived can be known, and to the extent that the concept of such a complex of judgements can be understood. This must also provide the explanation why facts which have very different structures can be the objects of historical science. Complexes of judgements, that is to say, theories, are always complexes determined by method, i.e. each of them has very specific preconditions corresponding to the organisation of its principle, to the function of its object. But however such a complex of judgement may be constituted – whether its purpose is to determine an object which has an artistic, religious, legal or natural character – to the extent that the complex follows from a principle it is itself the object of other judgements, of judgements of historical science. The historian has the right to say: because A is B, C is D, since his object must be incorporated in a complex of judgements which has the form: because A is B, C is D. Such a grounding judgement is therefore the logical form of the relationship in which every historical fact stands to every other. However elementary this idea might appear at first sight, the order which is concealed in the form of such a connection between two judgements is highly complex, and to understand the concepts of 'idea and individual', and therefore the concept of history, it is important to clarify this order.

The judgement: 'Because A is B, C is D', is intended to explain why C, the subject of the consequence, receives the determination D. First, the question is posed: 'What is C?' The determination: 'C is D' then follows from manifold considerations, namely, 'because A is B'. Such a determination must, however, necessarily follow from a principle. That which gives meaning to each individual judgement, 'A is B', 'C is D', etc., is its claim to be true, is the principle of validity. The judgement in which the reasons for something are expressed is also necessarily subject to the principle of validity. But the validity claimed in the latter case is for something other than in the former judgement; it is the validity of linking together two judgements as reason and consequence. Language distinguishes precisely here between the truth which a judgement claims for what is judged within it, between the correctness of a train of argument, and a statement which asserts that the linking of two judgements takes place of necessity, that it is subject to the principle of validity. Both – truth and correctness – therefore follow the same principle. They embody different manifestations of the same thing, which themselves stand in an unambiguous relationship to one another: on the correctness of a proof is based the claim to truth of that which follows from it.

Now, the judgement 'C is D' claims truth only for the single determination D of the subject C. Therefore, although the train of argument: 'Because A is B, C is D' has reached a relative conclusion in the judgement 'C is D', it must necessarily push further, since its goal is truth, i.e. the totality of the determinations of C. Its goal, incidentally, is also the totality of the determinations of A, B, D and of all the reasons for the correctness of this proof. And so the judgement 'C is D' in turn leads on to another question: 'What is E?'

It must be emphasised in the context of this discussion that not just anything deserves to be called a question. The inadequacy of an existing theory, of a system of judgements bound together as reason and consequence, when applied to something which cannot be grounded on the conditions of this theory, makes that something a problem, and the problem is therefore always the expression of a critique of an existing theory. The occasion for the question might well be accidental – although the concept and the possibility of such an accident would certainly be open to closer determination – but the meaning of the question is determined by the level of the theory from which it arises. The question must be well founded, i.e. correctly posed, on the basis of this theory. In the discussion of the grounds which first gave rise to the question, the concept of the object in question is gradually consolidated as the expression of the very specific conditions which the object satisfies – from the determinateness of the question to the determinateness of the answer. Just as the determinateness which the object takes on in a judgement is always relative, since it contains at the same time the indeterminateness of the object which the question which follows from that judgement seeks to determine, so also the indeterminateness of the object of the question is only relative, since it corresponds to the determinateness of the question.

Fundamentally, therefore, determinateness and indeterminateness are elements of every object-function, and the individual entity which is the bearer of such a function necessarily forms part of a chain, the links of which are connected together as reason and consequence. Within this chain it takes on its determinateness on its way from question to answer, and then in turn generates new links in the same way, as consequences. Anything which forms a link in such a chain – be it a judgement or a concept or some more complex relation which claims validity – takes on its determinateness as a function of its position in this series. No doubt, the object-function, and the way it is organised according to the methodical structure of the complex of reasons, is very diverse. More precisely, the structure of the judgements which are connected together in such a series is diverse, like the objects which attain determination through them.

The theoretical assumptions on which the question and then the answer are based are also determined by method. Or, which amounts to the same thing, the principle of all complexes of judgement, the idea of validity, is composed of ideas which, in terms of method, are of different types. But that all objects are subsumed under principles at the same time guarantees the unity of the order which gives expression to such conformity to principles, and which therefore expresses, despite all the differences, the relation to the idea. The idea itself is nothing other than the representative of a very specific order to which everything which claims validity, however different its structure might be, necessarily belongs. 'Because A is B, C is D' is the most elementary form in which this order becomes comprehensible; and it takes little more to reveal its more complex relationships.

Every judgement of the same type as: 'Because A is B, C is D' points, as it were, behind itself to a system of relatively determined reasons which are themselves bound together as reason and consequence. It points forward to a system of relatively undetermined judgements, likewise bound together as reason and consequence, which can be deduced from it. Each individual link in this order is therefore conditioned by a system of judgements which itself is conditioned in the same way. The only entity which is unconditioned, i.e. is not deducible from reasons, is the totality of the reasons for each individual link; this absolute totality is called the idea. To be sure, each individual link in this order is also a totality; for however incomplete something which a judgement pronounces valid may be, the judgement by which the validity is pronounced is, in terms of its form, a totality, to the extent that none of its parts can be detached from it without causing it, the other parts and the totality to become meaningless. But the totality of the individual link is only relative, and necessarily points to the idea as the absolute totality. Nevertheless, this very description of the idea gives rise to misgivings as to whether it could be a 'totality'. The idea would be a 'totality' if each of its individual links were the condition of every other.

Now, to be sure, the reason is always the condition of the consequence. But is the consequence the condition of the reason? Initially, everything seems to contradict this assumption. It can be readily understood that the judgement, 'because A is B, C is D', cannot be reversed. The judgement, 'because C is D, A is B', if the symbols had the same meaning, would be nonsense. Each of the two judgements, bound together as reason and consequence, is a function of its determinateness within the series, and it loses its meaning if it loses its position. If, therefore – as seems to follow from this – 'A is B' were a determinant of 'C is D' but 'C is D' were not a determinant for 'A is B', an assertion which has just been made, that each link in the series is a totality, would be refuted. Accordingly, the judgement, 'because A is B, C is D', would also have to be a totality as a single link in a series. It now appears, however, that although 'C is D' cannot be severed from 'A is B', 'A is B' can quite well be severed from 'C is D' without thereby changing its meaning. And if the judgement 'because A is B, C is D' is not a totality, the series of judgements bound together as reason and consequence also cannot be a totality. So what exactly is its status?

That grounding judgement states that 'C is D' is the consequence of 'A is B'. In this judgement, therefore, not only is the determination D obtained for the subject of the consequence C, but the reason 'A is B' also appears here as the determining factor of the determination 'C is D'. This is more clearly expressed in the judgement ('C is D') is the consequence of ('A is B'). And from here the possibility of a new judgement follows naturally. ('A is B') is the reason for ('C is D'), in which 'A is B' is determined by a relation to 'C is D'. Simple as this idea may be, it is a highly significant factor for the structure of every complex of reasons. First of all, it shows that in the judgement 'because A is B, C is D', all the individual parts are determinants for each other. It is therefore indeed a totality. However, 'C is D' is not only a determining factor of 'A is B' but is also co-determining for the whole system of reasons from which 'A is B' and finally 'C is D' follow. But to express this determinateness calls for a type of judgements which is no longer contained in the same dimension as 'A is B' and 'C is D'. If the determination whereby the judgements 'A is B' and 'C is D' impart their reasons to each other and then to the entire system, those judgements themselves become, as facts of a peculiar kind, as functions of their position within a complex of reasons, the object of a new judgement. For this reason the judgement 'because A is B, C is D', or, which amounts to the same thing, the judgements '('C is D') is the consequence of ('A is B')' and '('A is B') is the reason for ('C is D')' are judgements about judgements.

The analysis of the judgement 'because A is B, C is D' therefore leads to the definition of a type of judgement the purpose of which is to formulate the concept of an individual judgement and the totality of its reasons, that is, the concept of a complex of judgements – in short, a category of judgements about totalities, the purpose of which is to be valid. An investigation of these totalities would therefore be unable to disregard the fact that they are functions of validity. On the contrary, to investigate judgements means precisely to test their presuppositions, the legitimacy of their validity. The role of such higher judgements, such judgements about judgements, therefore becomes that of not being confined to supplying concepts for individual, relative totalities. Not only the totality of the judgements already deduced at a certain time forms part of such a complex of judgements, but also, because it is precisely the purpose of that complex to express timelessly valid truth and to be directed towards that truth as its goal, its principle; because the complex is necessarily driven towards questions and answers, towards a system of judgements not yet deduced, this system of not yet deduced judgements also forms part, as a determining factor, of the concept of that complex of judgements.

The investigation of judgements, of their structure, their validity, their specific methodological determinateness by means of higher judgements, therefore arrives at the determination of a concept of absolute totality which includes within itself the judgements together with their legitimate presuppositions. However, a determinate concept of the absolute totality of a complex of judgements is nothing other than a determinate concept of the truth of the validity (or of its methodologically determined functions) of nature, art, law, etc., – in short, a determinate concept of the idea. And because the determinate concept of this totality, as the outcome of the investigation of a complex of judgements, at the same time includes its conditioning presuppositions, it therefore supplies the determinate principle according to which judgements are deduced as consequences from that complex of judgements. It may therefore be said with justice that the consequence is deduced from a complex of judgements according to a determinate concept of the totality of this complex, according to a determinate concept of the idea. Each individual consequence, however, represents a determining factor not only for the relative totality of the system of its reasons, but forms in addition the new material which serves to determine the concept of the idea.

This gives rise to an unceasing interplay in which the idea determined by a consequence, being the principle of a complex of judgements, enlarges the concept of each individual judgement subordinate to it in accordance with this determination. It thus constantly impels the complex of judgements towards questions and answers and then, determined by the answers, initiates a new movement of the same kind. In other words, the order of the idea is a dialectical process, and anyone who investigates an individual element of this process must take into account not only the complex of judgements from which it followed but also the determinate concept of the idea according to which that element was deduced. And he will be unable to do so unless he understands the determinations which were imparted to the concept by that complex of judgements.

In short, the historian will need to understand the dialectical process of a totality when investigating an individual element within it. For – to state the matter explicitly – the dialectical process, encompassing everything that claims validity, is that particular order through which historical facts are connected to each other; it is the order of history. Its concept, and therefore the concept of each of its individual links, also includes as an invariant an element which has already been implicitly referred to in expressions such as 'judgements already deduced' and 'judgements not yet deduced', but the necessity of which has not yet been explicitly justified in this context. This element is the relation of the dialectical process to an 'I', or more precisely, to a community of 'I's, without which its order, and therefore the possibility of determining its progression in time, cannot be understood.

It was argued earlier that the judgement 'because A is B, C is D' is a totality only because, in a higher judgement, 'C is D', the consequence, can become a determining factor for 'A is B'. That founding judgement must therefore first be made by someone; and after it has been made it can itself become the object of an investigation for someone. Whether it is the same 'I' which first deduces such a judgement and then makes it the object of investigation, or whether it is different 'I's, the link in the dialectical process can be understood only as something which has been thought, and indeed, from the standpoint of the person making the judgement, as something which has been thought earlier. The judgement therefore proves to be an object with a very peculiar structure. The preconditions for its status as an object include the fact that it has been known, and that knowledge about this knowing is possible. It may therefore be said that the totality of the individual judgement, like that of the complex of judgements, is a function of the specific psychological regularity which is expressed by the series 'I know that I know, I know that I know that I know,' and so on.

Despite this dependence on a 'subjective' order, the totality is an object, and anything which is known is capable of an objective determination. That this is so is guaranteed by the possibility of determining 'something known' as a link in a dialectical process according to a principle, namely, according to the idea. A single regularity therefore encompasses the order of the 'I' and the order of the idea as correlative concepts, which would become meaningless in isolation from one another. It is the regularity of meaning; and it can therefore be stated that anything that has its place in a dialectical process is a meaning, determined in accordance with a judgement. The deduction of anything which is in any sense valid is bound to someone who is striving to know what is valid, to know the idea, by gradually cleansing what has not yet been determined, purging the determinateness of the question with the determinateness of the answer. He does this by using what has been thus derived as valid to determine in a concept the totality of the complex from which it has been derived. At the same time, however, the dialectical process reveals itself as a function of a temporal organisation to the person who, through his knowledge of something known, surveys the totality of a complex of judgements.

We referred earlier to judgements which are 'not yet determined' or are 'already determined'. This distinction has meaning only in relation to someone from whose perspective something is 'not yet deduced' or 'already deduced'. There must always be someone for whose consciousness links in the dialectical process which are 'already derived', 'already thought' are to be thought of as 'earlier', and for whom links 'not yet thought' are to be thought of as 'later' – that is, as earlier or later than his experience. There must be someone who can know about his experience and for whom, therefore, this experience is determined by the index 'now' in relation to everything past and future. The 'already thought' or the 'not yet thought' is determined as past or future in relation to the 'now', to what is currently thought. In other words, there must be someone for whom the totality of time-determined facts is a whole. If, then, every link in the dialectical process is necessarily associated with an experience, it follows that it must be experienced once, with the index 'now', and must therefore have an unambiguous relationship to time, i.e. to dimensional values by which the course of natural events is measured. The concept of an individual link in the dialectical process can be unambiguously understood only in combination with its relationship to an 'I' and to a location in time.

To sum up this idea: the time-determined, ego-related link in a dialectical process is nothing other than the object of the science of history. In this sense, which can no longer be misunderstood, the historical object is unique, as a function of its non-exchangeable position in a dialectical process. It is also non-recurring, in being a function of an ego which organises time, and in being co-ordinated with a particular place in measurable time. It is an 'individual'. And what was argued earlier about reason and consequence – that the reason determines the consequence, but that the consequence, as a reason, determines new consequences – applies also to the historical object. One individual determines and founds another, and does so according to a particular concept of the idea, which in turn is determined in part by the concept of the single individual. The relationships between idea and individual have therefore been clarified, at least to some extent, by the account of the dialectical process.

II

This inquiry set out from the question concerning the principle by which the historian selects what is historically valuable from the abundance of what has already been thought, experienced, accomplished. It was argued that such a principle could not – if research were indeed to serve truth – be brought in from outside history. The standards which the historian could use should be found within the structure of the course of history itself. It was only a different formulation of this same question which directed the inquiry towards the continuity of the course of history, the connection between the individual historical facts. Having formulated the problem in this way, we were able to derive from the experience offered by the study of art history a form of connection which appeared to be characteristic of historical objects in general: the connection between reason and consequence. Looking back now, we must ask whether the more detailed investigation has confirmed that assumption. It could have been pointed out at the outset that, just because something is a reason or a consequence, it is not therefore historical. Every manifestation of a person is, in some sense, founded on a reason. But no one will be of the opinion that all such manifestations are historical. It can certainly be said that they can become an object of history. There must therefore be certain standards according to which such manifestations are historical.

The question posed at the outset again impinges on our investigation in the form of a related problem. It can now be answered unequivocally: only that which someone derives as a consequence from reasons which have a claim to validity, and which therefore is in accordance with the idea, is an object of historical science. The conformity of something to the idea is therefore the precondition of its being an object of history. If there were some fears earlier that the term 'idea' might be ambiguous, after everything that has been said it is hoped that this term will no longer be misunderstood as a 'general law' for 'particular historical cases', or as some such dogma. The idea has meaning only as a principle and a representative of a dialectical process. We shall have to discuss in more detail the precise way in which an investigation of the dialectical process itself enables the researcher to recognise the idea by virtue of which he is then able to decide what is historically valuable. Something is an historical object of history, we said, through its relation to the idea. This 'something', however, is always a meaning, i.e. a function of the particular regularity which encompasses idea and ego as correlative orders indissolubly bound together.

It has already been pointed out that not all the manifestations of an ego, not everything which is a meaning, is for that reason historical. But because it is a meaning it must certainly in principle be historical, i.e. capable of being related to the idea. Historical objects, therefore – to state it once more in a different way – are always determined by judgements, i.e. by meanings which claim validity. And in this sense the judgement: 'because A is B, C is D' is indeed characteristic of the relationship between historical objects. Of course, the meanings linked together in that formulation must, as judgements, have an object. But whatever the nature of that object may be, the judgement about it is an object of historical science because it aims at validity, because it yields a determining factor for the idea. And the object of the judgement which is to be investigated by historical research will only become an object of historical research if it is itself a judgement, or is a relative or absolute totality of judgements which meet the preconditions which have been indicated.

This last observation gives an approximate idea of the extremely complex structure of the historical object, and therefore of the historical judgement. The object of historical investigation is a function of the idea in time; it is the dialectical process, together with all the individual totalities which are dialectically determined. Now, what does this definition of the object imply with regard to the structure of the historical judgement? It implies that only the order of the dialectical process, the necessity which informs its course, entitles the historian to link the object C to a determination D in a judgement. What the category is for the object of the natural sciences, namely the specific precondition of its determinateness as object, the dialectical process, or the idea, is for the historical object. The necessity of a connection established by the historical judgement between an object and its determination therefore follows from the principle of the idea. Nevertheless, this notion does no more than sketch the outlines of the structure of the historical judgement. What then, more precisely, is the procedure of historical research?

It has been shown that a meaning determined by a judgement, an ego-related, time-determined judgement, 'C is D', always presents itself as the object of historical investigation. The historian's task is to formulate the concept of this judgement. That is possible to the extent that the judgement is determined unambiguously as a function of its position in a dialectical process, or, to put it differently, as an element in a cultural field. For the system of culture is, in fact, nothing other than the time-related system of ideas. In performing this task the historian must keep two things in view: firstly, the particular reasons from which the judgement was deduced as a consequence; secondly, however, the particular concept of the idea according to which the deduction 'because A is B, C is D' was made. He cannot therefore elaborate the concept of an individual cultural fact, the meaning 'C is D', without taking account of judgements on judgements, namely the judgements in which a particular concept was formed of the totality of the cultural area to which the meaning 'C is D' belongs. He must take account, in other words, of the judgements in which a particular concept of the idea is formed. But the judgements in which that concept is formed, as judgements about time-determined and ego-related judgements, are elements of historical science. No element in the dialectical process of cultural areas is possible, therefore, without being related to historical science. It follows that historical research is bound up in a peculiar way with the dialectical process of the system of cultural areas.

This confronts our investigation, which aims at determining the structure of historical science more precisely, with the question: what is the relationship of historical research to all the other methodologically determined complexes of meaning? In other words, what is the position of historical research within the system of culture? This leads to a further question: all areas of validity – despite all the differences, which cannot be ignored, between, for example, art or law on the one hand and natural science on the other – are complexes of meaning determined by judgements, i.e. conforming to an idea, and are therefore, in the broadest sense of the term, sciences. That being so, what is the position of historical research within the system of sciences? To be sure, the system of those complexes of judgements which are based on knowledge of the truth of nature or history can – to repeat the point – be distinguished in a very definite way from all other complexes of judgements. In principle, however, it will at least no longer be possible to think of the relationships between that system, and the complexes of judgements which are directed at knowledge of the truth of beauty or law, in the earlier way, as if, within the system of areas of validity, the systems of art, science, law, etc., existed side-by-side, as it were, in separate dimensions. The system of areas of validity – which means nothing other than the idea – cannot be encompassed by a one-dimensional image. This statement must suffice here, since further discussion of this question must be left to a study concerned with the structure of the individual ideas. Only on that basis can the structure of the system of validity be discovered in all particular cases.

Here, only the role of historical science in this system is under discussion, and, to the extent that historical science is bound up with the multi-dimensionality of the system, we shall have to say more about it straight away. How, then, is historical research related to the system of culture? An example will make this relationship clear. Any general survey of the methods of natural science teaches us that its theory includes not only judgements directly concerned with determining the object of experience, but also judgements on the theory itself, for example, judgements on individual laws. The clear formulation of a problem, the determination of an object not yet determined, necessarily takes place within a continuous debate on the theoretical premises of the objects already determined. Anyone who wishes to master a new case will have to form judgements on those earlier objects from the point of view of the new case. However, a particular theory, or particular laws, can only be objects because they are links in a dialectical process. Determination of them is therefore subject to the methodological premises of historical research. That is the justification for saying that judgements in historical research necessarily form part of the theoretical content of natural science. When individual theorems and individual laws are cited together with the names of their authors in discussions within the natural sciences, therefore, that is not merely a technical adjunct, but a requirement of the matter itself. We are concerned here with objects for the concepts of which ego and time are necessary reference points. No doubt the law has timeless validity; no doubt it was valid, if one might put it thus, before it was determined. But to the extent that it is a meaning determined by judgement it is 'historical', an object of historical science.

Now, to characterise a judgement about a law as a judgement of historical science is in no way to deny that it forms part of natural science. Every judgement which makes possible a debate between individual theorems of natural science serves in its own way to advance the knowledge of the natural object. It may therefore be said that particular judgements of historical science can be utilised in the same way as knowledge of nature. It will be understood that this 'utilisation' does not depend on an arbitrarily chosen purpose, but is called for by the task of the natural sciences. Judgements of historical science utilised for the purposes of the natural sciences give expression to the determination which is added by the solution of the individual problem – the individual consequence deduced from reasons – to theory within the dialectical process, and therefore to the idea of 'nature'. They therefore make it possible for new problems and new consequences to be derived from theory according to the ever-renewed determination of the concept.

It would not be without value to recall, at this point in the investigation, the example from the history of mechanics used earlier to elucidate the problem of totality. What could not be fully understood at that stage, the reason why an example from history was used to investigate the relationship between individual laws as links in a totality, find its answer in these later considerations. There is also a further reason for referring back to those ideas at this point. For it is from this perspective in particular that one can explain why the problem of judgement, the problem of totality, provides the starting point for refuting the opinion which is inclined to see the logical forms of the knowledge of nature as the forms of knowledge as such. Precisely the notion of a functional connection between history and the natural sciences, which follows from the analysis of the concept of totality, makes it possible to define unambiguously the limits set to the knowledge of nature, the limits of concept formation within the natural sciences.

At the same time, if we pursue these thoughts in other directions, we can see clearly where the limits of the historical method are to be sought; in other words, we can establish the position of historical research within the system of culture. What has been demonstrated here with regard to the natural sciences applies no less to the relationship of historical research to all the other dialectically advancing complexes of judgements. To the extent that judgements about judgements have their place in every such complex, the complex advances according to an idea, and is connected to the science of history in the same way as are the natural sciences.

The task of every historical investigation necessarily extends over several dimensions of the dialectical process. Firstly, it is directed at a particular individual fact; then it has to test the idea according to which that fact has been derived and, thirdly, it has to investigate the premises of this particular concept of the idea, i.e. the premises of certain historical judgements. Only then – and precisely this is its purpose – does the historical investigation encompass the entire movement of the dialectical process. If, for example, the historian faces the task of understanding a fact relating to the medieval view of nature, he will first seek to establish the individual grounds from which it was deduced. He will be unable to do this without taking account of the particular concept of the idea of 'nature', and he is therefore compelled to investigate the premises of the medieval concept of the idea, and therefore the structure of the judgements in which this concept was formulated, the structure of medieval historical research.

To plumb the furthest depths of the dialectical process in this way is not a requirement that he can meet; nor, however, can he escape it as he pleases. For it is only by keeping the totality of the dialectical movement in view in this way that he can do justice to the individual historical fact. This enables us to recognise, at the same time, the justification for the historian's actual behaviour, in believing that an individual fact must always also be understood as an element of a particular epoch, and in feeling obliged to understand the fact not only from its position within the dialectic of one field of objects – for example, a work of art within the dialectic of art – but also to see it in relation to the ideas of nature, religion, law, morality, etc., which were characteristic of that people. It is the unity of the assumptions to which the concepts of the ideas are subject at any time which makes this procedure possible. In this way the complexion of the dialectical process reveals itself from a new aspect. To be sure, an individual fact of law or of the natural sciences does not intervene directly in the processes of the other fields. But because the individual fact co-determines its idea and, more widely, the idea itself, it also influences, through the detour of the concept of the idea, all the other fields of objects. Because all the individual fields of culture are related together in this way, a single dialectical movement embraces the entire system of culture.

The unity of the premises of the concept of the idea to which the historian must gain access if he wishes to understand his object in its full extent is nothing other than the unity of the principle by which the concept of the idea is determined again and again by each individual fact in historical judgements, the principle by which historical judgements are derived as consequences from reasons. Now this principle is the idea of the system of ideas or – it will no longer be possible to misunderstand this expression – the idea of the idea. That is not to say that two different ideas stand, as it were, one above the other, but that this phrase is only an expression for the multi-dimensionality of the idea as a unity, a totality which necessarily belongs to the series: 'I know, I know that I know, etc.'

Such considerations again provide vantage points from which the position of historical research within the system of culture can be understood. There is no object of historical research – so it has been argued in all these reflections – which does not confront the historian with the necessity of reflecting on the principle of his own procedure. It therefore becomes impossible to differentiate between the science of history and the philosophy of history. Historical research is a science of principles, is philosophy, in that it cannot investigate the individual historical fact without considering the idea underlying this fact, without taking account of the principle of the judgements in which the concept of the idea comes into being, and therefore without testing the premises of its own method. Certainly, historical research is an empirical science, since its object is a time-determined fact. But because of the peculiar structure of this object, for historical research, unlike the natural sciences, the distinction between empirical science and the science of principles falls away.

Nor is one entitled to say that, to the extent that historical research relates to time-determined facts, it is an empirical science, while to the extent that it investigates the multi-dimensional structure of the idea it is a doctrine of principles. As will become clear more vividly later, the peculiar structure of this empirical 'experience' makes such a distinction impossible. Nor will it be possible to sustain the view that the science of history, though it may in some respects be a science of principles, constitutes, as the philosophy of history, one department, as it were, of philosophy, which has its place beside other departments such as the philosophy of law, of nature, and so on. There is fundamentally no possibility of indicating a point at which philosophy stops being historical philosophy. Clearly, we are concerned here with the fundamental possibility of such a distinction between philosophy and historical science, not with a question of fact. Nevertheless, to clarify this question some further reflection is needed.

The claim to be a science of principles has now been sustained with regard to historical science. If that assertion is justified, it is now necessary to substantiate the same claim with regard to philosophy. An analysis of the method of philosophy or, to put it differently, of the dialectical process of the science of principles, will provide an answer to the question whether a distinction between philosophy and historical science is possible. The path of the investigation therefore leads back into the midst of the workings of the dialectical process, and does so now at the level, so to speak, of its highest dimension, that of the dialectical process of the science of principles.

The objects of philosophy are all those relations which lay claim to validity, in a word: judgements. These present themselves as the results of research in the broadest sense of the term, research being understood as the totality of the actions directed at gaining knowledge of the idea. The task of philosophy is not exhausted if it contents itself with considering an individual period of research, even the one closest in time. In principle, it is the totality of the process of the system of culture, which for the present of historical research is 'past', which should provide philosophical investigation with its material. Thus, it emerges that philosophy has at least the same material, the same objects, as history. But do not the methods of investigation of the two disciplines now diverge? The task of historical research, it has been argued, is to formulate the concept of a historical fact, of a dialectically determined totality. Philosophy by contrast, it might be said, has to do merely with the claim of such a fact to validity. Its task is to investigate this claim to validity, the timeless validity of that fact. If, therefore, the concept of a judgement can be determined without testing the legitimacy of its claim to validity, and if, conversely, the legitimacy of a claim to validity can be tested without at the same time determining the concept of a historical fact, of a judgement which has its place in a dialectical process, then history and philosophy are indeed different disciplines.

However, such a distinction between empirical science and the historical science of principles is not possible – to formulate the matter definitively – because the historical object is an 'empirical object' only as the bearer of a claim to validity. Just as its claim to timeless validity cannot be severed from the meaning of the fact of the 'judgement', just as the concept of the judgement cannot be formulated without testing its claim to validity, and just as, conversely, this claim cannot be tested without determining the concept of a fact, so, finally, history cannot be separated from philosophy. Their method, the dialectical process of the science of principles, therefore takes the following path, assuming that the task is to investigate the object 'C is D'.

By investigating the claim of this object to validity the researcher determines it historical value. He can test this claim to validity only by testing at the same time the reasons from which 'C is D' was deduced, by seeking to understand the idea according to which it was deduced. If, for example, he has in view a certain concept of the idea of 'nature', of the kind which has attained determination within a system of historical judgements – which, up to now, we have called philosophical judgements – he must now advance yet further and test the principle to which that system is subject, the idea of the idea, the idea of the system of validity, and therefore the premises of his own discipline. This idea, however, will in each case receive its determination from the particular concepts of the idea as formulated by the science of principles in its investigation of the individual historical fact. It will then, in its turn, once more determine the already determined concepts of the idea, in their full depth, with all their functions and over the full length of the dialectical process, with regard to their rightful claim to validity.

In this way the science of principles, in its dialectical process, reviews its own principles as historically determined facts, the validity of which must be proved. Only by doing so will it become a critical science of history in the true sense of the word. As long as it defends itself with rigid and 'absolute' principles against the influence which autonomously acquired knowledge must necessarily have on its own procedure – as long as it closes its eyes to the perception that *its* principle, too, claims timeless validity (although, as an element of the dialectical process, it is time-determined and ego-related, and is therefore a *relative* concept of the absolute totality) – its efforts will remain fruitless. Only when it constantly tests against experience the standards by which it accords validity to certain meanings from the abundance of meanings, thereby adjudging them 'historical', will it be a critical science of history.

Such considerations give access at the same time to another much-discussed problem, the question of the relationship between psychology and history. It has been shown that every meaning becomes 'historical' when it has its place in the dialectical process, the principle of which is the idea. Conversely, something is an object of history only as meaning, i.e. when it has a relation to an 'I'. If it is asked, therefore, with what right an 'I' belongs to history, and what provides the measuring rod for the value of an 'I', one would answer first of all as follows: It is not only the case that the 'I' provides a reference point for the concept of the dialectically determined meaning; but also a system of such meanings must necessarily be capable of becoming a determining factor for the 'I'. By virtue of this determination, therefore, the concept of an 'I' can also be formulated.

This should not be misunderstood. If one speaks of the determined concept of an 'I', this idea cannot be an attempt to relationise the 'I'. The singularity, and in this sense the relationlessness, of the 'I' results inalienably from the fact that it must be capable of assignment to every kind of relation as the entity whereby the relation is realised, as the absolutely unique entity which experiences every relational context. The 'I', as the subject of experience, as the centre of a temporal articulation, as the bearer of the series: 'I know that I know, I know that I know that I know', is situated in a dimension of its own, which is necessarily correlated to each of the dimensions of the dialectical process.

But by saying: 'I know myself', one expresses at the same time the fact that the 'I' can be experienced in a dimension different from that just described, i.e. must be capable of being determined by relations. Just as the series: 'I know that I know, etc.,' includes knowledge of oneself, and just as I can only know myself because I am this determined 'I' clearly distinguished from others, so the necessity of a plurality of 'I's, which stand in an unambiguous relation to one another through their connection to objectively determinable meanings – that is, through their relation to the idea – follows from the series of knowledge, from the very structure of the 'I'.

Thus, the series of knowledge itself requires, on the one hand, the singularity of the 'I', but on the other a multiplicity of 'I's which are objectively determinable as 'yous' and which, through their relation to the idea, must be capable of being objects of historical research – in short, it requires a community of 'I's. The matter can also be stated as follows: on the one hand, the 'I' experiences and articulates time, but, on the other, experience, and therefore the experiencing subject, exist in time. Finally, the 'I' can in turn experience itself, along with its temporal determinateness. This is nothing other than a variation of the series of knowledge, now in relation to time. The 'I', which experiences something, and in so doing is the centre of an articulation of time, is undoubtedly one with the 'I' which has its place in the community or, which amounts to the same thing, in time, and can therefore be determined as an object. Obviously, however, the location from which the 'I' is judged to be an experiencing subject is different from the location from which it is judged to be a time-determined object.

To put it briefly, one makes the former judgement as a psychologist, the latter as an historian. To speak of a necessary co-ordination between history and psychology would therefore be to say too little. The historian will never be able to abstain from 'placing himself in someone's shoes', while the psychologist will never be able to disregard the fact that he is dealing with optimal, individual relations. According to the series: 'I know that I know', the experiencing 'I' confronts itself in a second dimension as a 'you' which is objectively determinable within a community, and then finally confronts itself on the next rung as the 'I' which experiences that 'you'. According to this series the psychologist and the historian differ not in their object, which is the same for both, but in the dimension within which they apprehend this object.

The interpenetration of the two disciplines is clarified by a further idea: common to both is the fact that they do not 'know' their object, but rather 'understand' it. Linguistic usage distinguishes these terms in a peculiar way. Both 'to know' and 'to understand' give expression to the orientation of an 'I' to an object; both appear in the guise of a judgement. But 'to understand', unlike 'to know', relates to an object which is an 'object' only to the extent that, and because, it is related to an 'I'. Something can only be understood, therefore, if it conforms to a principle by virtue of which it is an object which is at the same time ego-related and time-determined. This explains why 'to understand' always refers to two modes of operation: 'to understand' someone and 'to understand' something. Just as one cannot understand 'something' without at the same time under-standing 'someone', or 'someone' without 'something', in just the same way psychology cannot be distinguished from history.

This thought leads to the heart of the question of the objective determinability of an 'I'. One precondition for this determinability is, first of all, a multiplicity of 'I's. This multiplicity was shown earlier to be required by the series of knowledge itself. A second precondition, however, is a principle by which the individual 'I' is distinguished from others within this multiplicity. Such an objectively valid principle is likewise required by that series, for I cannot know myself, I 'am' not, unless I am unambiguously related to other 'I's, am distinguished from them. I can only understand myself at all if I mean by 'myself', at the same time, 'something' – that which is thought by me – which must be understandable in the same way by everyone. That I am unambiguously determinable as a member of a community, as the 'someone' who is understood in that which is thought by me, I owe to the principle from which follows the unambiguity of that which is thought by me. Earlier, the necessity of the idea's relation to an 'I' was demonstrated in relation to the idea; the same thing has now been shown in relation to the 'I'. But while the earlier argument dealt with the correlation of the idea with an 'I' in absolute terms, this notion is now given a new twist by the substitution for the 'I' of a community of 'I's. What does this correlativity mean for the concept of the idea and for the concept of community?

One thing emerges clearly from what has been said so far: the multiplicity of 'I's is a community because each 'I' must fundamentally be able to communicate with others. The principle by which 'something' is valid for every 'I' is the principle of communication. It is therefore also the principle of community. That unambiguous relations – which guarantee the objective determinability of the 'I' – are possible between 'I's, is due to that principle alone. However, this objective determinability, this objectivity of the 'I', because it concerns a 'subject', an 'I', is a different matter from the objectivity of all other objects. The 'I' must know about the idea, the principle of its own determinability, and determine itself accordingly in a peculiar sense. How, then, does this 'self-determination' of the 'I' proceed?

The first point to be made is that the 'I' cannot know itself or determine the way in which it is without determining, with the same thought, the way in which it was and will be. For it is 'I' only as the centre of a temporal articulation, in so far as it understands the 'now', in which it currently is, to be 'not earlier' and 'not later' – in so far, therefore, as it thinks simultaneously its 'now', its 'earlier' and its 'later'. In other words, it can think itself only as a totality in which these three phases reciprocally determine each other. When the 'I' investigates how it was, at the same time it determines the reasons why it has become as it is now and not otherwise. This 'now' can only be understood as the future of the 'I' which has become present, the direction of which is determined not only by reasons from which it has followed, but also by the principle according to which the 'I' has brought about this present, i.e. this wholly determined system of relations to others. For it is the characteristic function of this principle to specify to the 'I' what its relations to other 'I's must be, i.e. what they will be in the future, if they are to claim validity for everyone, for the community.

Every 'I' must therefore always be able to derive its own future according to this principle accessible to its knowledge – according to the idea. And it is the function of the idea to determine not only how something must be, but also how an 'I', how the community must be. Indeed, one can only say of something that 'it must be' to the extent that, and because, it is a determining factor for an 'I', a relation between this 'I' and other 'I's. For 'must' is the expression of the validity-adequacy of something which is to be understood as a consequence of reasons. This is because the idea is the guideline for the behaviour of the 'I' which deduces the consequence, and because the consequence deduced, in being intended to be valid for the community, represents a relation between the 'I' which deduces and every other possible 'I'.

Conversely, the phrase 'I want to do something' expresses the idea that it is always a very definite 'I' which determines, on the basis of its present, its future relations to other 'I's. In view of these considerations, the absolute totality of the complexes of meanings determined by judgements, the idea, has the function of being the totality of the relations between 'I' and 'I'. Thus, one of the functions of the idea is to be the idea of the community or, which amounts to the same thing, to be the idea of the good, i.e. the standard by which the 'I' is to regulate its behaviour towards others, and according to which the 'wanting' of the 'I' is capable of objectivity determination.

I said earlier that each historical fact is a determining factor for an 'I'. That idea can now be explicated to mean that the fact, in the broadest sense of the term, is an 'action', a deed or a work. An 'I' must have been confronted by the question: How must I act? The action will be historical if the standard by which the 'I' regulates its actions is valid for everyone, i.e. for the community. The idea of the community, therefore, is not an individual subdivision of the idea, like the idea of art, law and other methodologically determined ideas. Rather, it expresses the idea that validity is always validity for someone, and that this someone, because of his correlation to 'something' which is valid for him – but also, in a certain sense, is always valid even without regard to him – is also capable of objective determination. In other words, he obeys an idea as the principle of his determination. This idea, the idea of community, is therefore just as richly articulated methodologically as the 'something' which is valid for the community, as the idea in general. That is the reason why the image of juxtaposition cannot reproduce the position of the idea of the community within the system of ideas, but only the image of a dimension.

The latter image – to repeat the point once more – expresses the fact that all the functions of the idea must also be able to be seen as relations between 'I's, as actions, while the actions in their turn, the functions of the idea of 'community', are determined methodologically in no less manifold ways than the 'something' which the subject of the action sets as the goal of his action. The idea of community as a dimension of the idea in general makes it possible fundamentally to regard the totality of the dialectically advancing cultural areas at the same time as a totality of complexes of actions. The relation between 'I's is an action, in so far as it obeys an idea as its standard.

As a result of all these considerations, our investigation is now confronted by a new aspect of the dialectical process: the function of the idea of 'community' in time. It must therefore be possible straight away to determine the position of historical science within the system of culture from a new aspect. This new aspect concerns the relationship of history to ethics.

Our train of thought led directly from the problem of the relations between psychology and history to a discussion of the problem of the objective determinability of the 'I'. As the precondition for such determinability the idea was mentioned, in its function of being the idea of community. This idea, it was argued, is the standard by which the 'I' must regulate itself in its relations to other 'I's, and therefore in its actions. The 'I' is unambiguously determinable because, as the subject of actions, it can regulate itself according to this idea, and the rightness and value of its behaviour can be tested according to it. The investigation of the relations between history and psychology therefore leads directly to the problem of the relation of history to ethics. After all that has been said up to now, this problem can be formulated briefly in the questions: Is every action which conforms to duty, i.e. which meets the conditions of the idea of 'community', already for that reason 'historical'? Does it form part of the dialectical process of history simply through its relation to the idea?

To answer these questions exhaustively it would be necessary to look more deeply into the structure of society . . . [9]

[End of extant typescript]

---

9 The original dissertation typescript ends on p. 54 with this incomplete sentence. On the cover page a note in square brackets in Elias's handwriting says 'pages 55–57 missing'. See Note on the text, p. xiv.

4

Idea and individual: A contribution to the philosophy of history

Summary of a doctoral thesis for the Faculty of Philosophy of the Schlesische Friedrich-Wilhelms-Universität, Breslau; doctorate awarded 30 January 1924.

Supervisor: Professor Dr Hönigswald
Oral examination: 26 July 1922

The problem of the individual is posed by the realisation that there are facts which cannot be determined by the methods of the natural sciences. There are objects which stand in a relationship to the conditions to which they owe the possibility of conceptual definition which is unlike the relationship of the particular case to the general law. This is, to begin with, a merely negative observation, but it implies that the specific structure of such objects, which are not conditioned by 'laws', should be explored in greater depth.

Seen in this light, the concept of the individual takes on a significance which goes beyond the customary limitation to persons, to 'I's. It appears as the representative of an order, and therefore of everything which conforms to this order. This order reveals itself in the discipline of history. The task, therefore, is to investigate the lawfulness to which that discipline conforms.

Every historical fact is characterised by a place in time. In other words, it must be associated with a natural event. Time, or the natural event, therefore emerges as one of the invariants[1] in relation to which the

Translation of 'Idee und Individuum: Ein Beitrag zur Philosophie der Geschichte', Auszug aus einer Schrift zur Erlangung der Doktorwürde der Hohen Philosophischen Fakultät der Schles. Friedrich-Wilhelms-Universität zu Breslau, Breslau, Hochschulverlag Breslau, 1924.

1 N.B. The three invariants mentioned in this document all contradict statements made in Elias's doctoral thesis itself. See the Note on the text, p. xiv for an explanation of how this came about.

historical fact receives its determinateness. Of what kind, therefore, is the relationship of historical factuality to the natural event?

To put it briefly: the meaning an event takes on under certain conditions in someone's experience determines that event as historical. Unlike physical time, therefore, historical time expresses the relationship of an event to certain experiences.

It is true that not all experiences are as such historical. But to the extent that historical factuality appears to be linked to the concept of experience, to the extent that it is a meaning-structure, the subject of experience, the 'I', which 'experiences something' in unambiguous relationship to a natural event, is to be considered the *second* invariant of the historical fact.

Historical facts are therefore conditioned by those experiences which are distinguished from all others by their relationship to certain principles. However, as an experience which obeys certain principles, the historical event has a right to claim validity for all.

To be sure, no meaning-structure which lacks any relationship to norms is fundamentally possible. However, it will be conceded, at the least, that every meaning-structure *can* be related to norms. Of all meaning-structures, only those which meet the requirement of conforming to norms belong to the system of history. Or it may be said that a meaning-structure forms part of history if its conformity to norms and its claim to validity are proven. There follow from this certain conclusions regarding the relationship of history to historical science, but, above all, the important requirement of validity, which is satisfied by the historical fact. This validity constitutes the *third* invariant.

At the same time, however, the problems of the individual and of history can be pursued in many different directions from this perspective.

On the nature of the relationship that connects the condition and the conditioned within historical science the following may now be stated:

Every historical fact must be derived, in accordance with an idea, from 'reasons', as a meaning-structure which has a claim to validity. These reasons, which also have a claim to validity, refer back behind them to a system of relatively determined meaning-structures from which they themselves have in their turn been derived as consequences. The most elementary form which expresses the organisation of all systems that can be referred to as historical is therefore the judgement: 'Because A is B, C is D'. Such a grounding judgement expresses that 'C–D' is the consequence of 'A–B'. In such a judgement, therefore, not only is the determination D obtained for the subject of the consequence C, but at the same time the reason 'A–B' appears here as the determining factor of the determinateness 'C is D'. This is expressed more clearly in the judgement '(C–D) is the consequence of (A–B)'. This now yields without further derivation the possibility of a new judgement: 'A is B' is the reason for 'C is D', since 'A is B', the reason, is determined by its relation to 'C is D', the consequence. It will be possible to go still further: 'C is D' is not only a determining factor of 'A is B' but is co-determining of the whole system of reasons from which 'A is B' and, finally, 'C is D' themselves followed. This process, in which a consequence follows from reasons, a new meaning of the reasons follows from the consequence and, finally, new consequences subject to the same order are generated – this dialectical process characterises the interrelationship of historical facts. At the same time, the exposition of this process provides the answer to the question as to the specific conditionality of the historical fact. This fact appears as conditioned by the system of reasons from which it was derived according to a principle. It is further conditioned by a system of consequences which follow from it. In short, it is a function of its position within a dialectically driven system of meaning-structures, and indeed, of meaning-structures which, as bearers of a claim to validity, obey the idea of validity as their principle.

Although the particular individual idea, according to which something is derived as a consequence from reasons, may be a historical concept and therefore itself subject to the laws of the dialectical process, the idea of validity as a principle of the dialectical process is exempt from the movement of that process. It is an expression of the unity and the unchanged identity of this order of the dialectical process, as functions of which process meaning-structures receive their determinateness. By virtue of this unity of the ordering principle of validity, in relation to which the historical process appears as an order, it is therefore possible in principle to speak of a science of history and of an historical truth.

5

Anecdotes

In addition to great and momentous events, historiography often passes down to us incidents of no importance to the course of history – a brief scene, perhaps only a word. Such little scenes may, however, bring so vividly before our eyes a question relating to the eternal play of human life that, taken on their own, lifted from the flux of history, they delight our minds as little gems conceived by the fertile imagination of a demiurge.

These immortal anecdotes from antiquity again and again become topical in some new way for each generation. I shall relate a few of them, gleaned from my reading of ancient writers.

I *Aristides and money*[1]

Aristides was a man of the highest statesmanship who guided the fate of the Athenian people over a long period. The following incident tells us how he thought about money.

A close relation of his, a rich merchant called Callias, once had serious accusations made against him by his enemies. After setting out all the points of their complaint, his accusers added this further argument: 'You all know Aristides, the son of Lysimachus, who is admired by the whole of Greece', they said. 'How do you think things look in his household, when you see him appear in public in his old, threadbare coat? Should we not suppose that this man, who freezes in public, also goes hungry at home and wants for everything? What, then, do you think of a man such as Callias, the

Translation of 'Anekdoten', *Berliner Illustrirte Zeitung* 33: 29 (20 July 1924), pp. 811–22. [Published under the name of Dr Michael Elias]

1 For this story, Elias drew upon Plutarch, *Lives*, Aristides, xxv. (See, for example, the Loeb Classical Library edn, trans. B. Perrin (Cambridge, MA: Harvard University Press, 1914), vol. II, pp. 290–3).

richest citizen of Athens, who allows his kinsman with wife and children to go short, while he has enjoyed so many advantages from Aristides' good reputation?'

When Callias saw that this reproach most angered the judges, he had Aristides sent for and asked him to attest before the judges that he, Aristides, had rejected every request Callias had made to support him, every plea to help him.

Aristides stepped before the court in his modest way and said that he had indeed rejected all offers of support from Callias, since he did not need them.

He then went on to say:

'There are many rich men among us, and that is to our benefit, since it is from them that the state derives its greatest revenues.

'But as far as the statesman is concerned, in whose hands public welfare is placed, it is my opinion that he should really be obliged to give away his wealth before taking up state office. For I do not believe that anyone can be mindful, at the same time, of the prosperity of the state and of preserving his own wealth.

'You may think this judgement too harsh. But you will at least agree with me that the man who takes over the management of public affairs without wealth and hands it to his successor as a wealthy man is to be condemned. The people could never give that man what the leader of the state needs most of all, *its trust* – the confidence that in all cases he will give the state's advantage precedence over his own.

'The merchant has to earn and increase his wealth. That is his profession, and if he does not increase his wealth he is a bad merchant. It is therefore absurd to accuse this man', and he pointed to Callias, 'of earning too much.

'The finest and most honourable things that can be said of a statesman are, first, that he has guided the state judiciously in difficult times, but, second, that he has remained poor, although as a ruler he had power and influence enough to divert money into his own pocket.

'That is the reason why I have always rejected my cousin Callias' kind offers, and will always reject such offers in future.

'Others may have a different opinion. I, at least, took up my office in this coat, and I shall not leave it in a better one.'

Thus spoke Aristides, the Athenian.

2   The judgement of the shards [2]

A great fear of the Athenians was that one of their leaders might use his power and influence to overthrow the democratic constitution and seize autocratic control of the Athenian state.

They therefore established the following institution: if there was a desire to be rid of an influential man for the reason mentioned above, or perhaps for other reasons, the so-called judgement of the shards could be used against him. According to this practice, each citizen took a shard,[3] wrote on it the name of the man he wanted to see removed from the city and took it to a place enclosed by barriers in the middle of the market-place. The man whose name appeared on the most shards was exiled from the city for ten years.

When a vote was taken in this way on Aristides, whose justness and pure sentiments were known to all, but whose opponents feared that for this very reason he might gain too much influence, it is told that a farmer from the rural parts of Athens gave his shard to Aristides, who was standing next to him, and asked him to write the name 'Aristides' on it. The latter asked him in astonishment whether Aristides had done him any harm. 'Not at all', answered the little farmer, 'I don't even know the man, but it annoys me that everyone has his name on their lips and calls him 'the just', as if there were no honest people apart from him.'

Aristides wrote his name on the shard in silence and the farmer placed it with the others.

Not long afterwards Aristides left Athens as an exile.

3   Alexander and the statue of the man clapping his hands [4]

The Macedonians, farmers and sons of farmers, led by Alexander the Great and the flower of the Macedonian nobility, were about to complete the conquest of Asia Minor. The Macedonian army observed the curiosities

2   Elias took this story from Plutarch's *Lives*, Aristides, VII (Loeb edn, II, pp. 230–5.)

3   A piece of earthenware.

4   This story from Alexander's campaigns has been passed down in various versions. Elias appears to have drawn mainly on the celebrated history of the conqueror's exploits by Arrian (Lucius Flavius Arrianus) probably supplemented from other sources. See Arrian, *History of Alexander*, II, 5. 1–4. (See, for example, Loeb Classical Library edn, trans. P. A. Brunt (Cambridge, MA: Harvard University Press, 1976), vol. I, pp. 136–9.)

of the Asiatic world with childlike, ever-growing astonishment. Until shortly before, the majority of the soldiers had known little more than the district of their native village, and only a small noble upper stratum had come into close contact with the subtleties of Greek culture.

In their advance through Asia Minor the Macedonians – a young people, strong, courageous and full of confidence – had reached Tarsus and then Anchialus, towns situated on the southern coast of Asia Minor, roughly opposite the eastern tip of Cyprus. They set up quarters at Anchialus. There a few soldiers who were walking about the town looking at anything worth seeing discovered a curious statue on the foundations of the town wall. It depicted a man who appeared to be in the act of clapping his hands. Below it was an inscription in characters unknown to the Macedonians.[5]

Alexander was told about it and he, too, came to look at the statue. He asked the inhabitants who had gathered around him and his soldiers whom this statue represented and what the inscription meant. They sent for an Assyrian priest who, they said, knew about the statue, and from him Alexander learned the following.

In earlier times, said the priest, the Assyrians had held dominion over most of the territories which now belonged to the Persians and which, it seemed, Alexander intended to conquer. At the head of their mighty armies the Assyrian kings had marched triumphantly through all these lands. They divided the conquered regions into administrative districts, towns were founded, arts and sciences flourished. Then the administration loosened, the kings and authorities grew lax and tired and the Assyrian empire fell victim to stronger peoples. The Babylonians rebelled, the Medes won victories throughout the land and made it their own. Then the same thing happened to them as to their predecessors. The Persians came down from their mountains and took possession of the whole country.

'This piece of stonework', said the priest, 'is the tomb of the Assyrian king Sardanapalus. He himself is depicted on it as if about to clap his hands, and what this means can be seen from the verses written underneath.'

As he said this, the priest took a few steps towards Alexander and fixed him with his eye:

'The inscription', he said, 'says the following:

5 Cuneiform writing.

Sardanapalus, son of Anakyndaraxes,
founded Anchialus and Tarsus in one day.
You, however, stranger passing by,
Eat, drink and be merry, for all the rest,
All that men possess and plan and build,
Is worth not even as much as the fleeting sound
Of the clapping of these poor hands.'

By 'be merry', however, it is reported that something much more frivolous was expressed in the Assyrian tongue.

As he spoke the last line the priest clapped his hands softly once, as if he wanted to bring the movement of the statue to its end. Then, without wasting another word, he went his way, as if not the slightest thing was left to be said.

The Macedonian soldiers heard and saw all this with some astonishment. Alexander himself is said to have gone away a pensive man. But then he moved on, and not long afterwards he and his exultant army defeated the Persian king at Issus, conquered Egypt, finally defeated the Persians at Guagamela and marched, fighting, conquering and winning victories in Assyria, Babylon and Media, through the whole of present-day Persia as far as India. He turned back at the Indus and died on his homeward journey in Babylon, full of new plans.

4   Victor and vanquished [6]

Although the man who finally conquered Alexander the Great's homeland, Macedonia, was not a Greek, he was a Roman of the best sort, Lucius Aemilius Paulus. He was intelligent and not without greatness, and his thinking was clear, precise and just.

By contrast Perseus, the last king of Macedonia, who occupied Alexander's throne, was weak rather than bad; but – and this was worse – he had about him an odour of avarice and cowardice.

He was not much loved.

---

6   The source of this story is Plutarch, *Lives*, Aemilius Paulus, XXVI–XXVII (Loeb edn, vol. VI, pp. 422–9).

Nevertheless, the Macedonians, who had to defend their homeland in any case, fought bravely against the Roman army under the leadership of the aged Aemilius Paulus. Only with difficulty was he able to subdue the Macedonians, force them to yield and finally to flee. One of the first who sought safety was the king himself. He lost his way, accompanied by a few friends. He discarded his purple cloak to be less easily recognised. He dismounted from his horse to be closer to those accompanying him; but he could not prevent one of them hanging back to fasten his sandal, another to water his horse, a third to quench his thirst.

Finally, abandoned by everyone and filled with fear and dread, he was barely able to hide from the Roman troops, who were hard on his heels and were increasingly encircling him. Finally, having no way out, he gave himself up to a Roman patrol which had run him to earth. Immediately, he begged to be taken to Aemilius Paulus. The Roman leader was accustomed to treat even his defeated foe with decency and respect, for by showing respect to the vanquished he rightly believed he earned still greater respect for himself. Above all, however, a man like Aemilius Paulus owed to his upbringing, in addition to all the other advantages, the virtue of tact. He was therefore genuinely concerned to spare the vanquished king any needless affront. Shocked by the fate of his adversary who, in a few days, had sunk from being a king ruling over thousands to a man amounting to less than nothing, he rose at once from his seat, as Perseus in wretched attire and a lamentable state of mind was brought into his tent. As he approached the king the Roman was hardly able to restrain his tears. But Perseus, in a frenzy of fear for his life, threw himself to the ground before Aemilius Paulus and, clasping his knees, could do no better than beg for his life with unseemly, cowardly words.

Paulus, who had been ready to meet the king in kingly fashion, could not long endure the sight of the whimpering wretch. He tried to calm him, but when Perseus, the heir of Alexander the Great, cried out and wailed that he would not get up until Aemilius had promised that no harm would come to him, the Roman said with a sorrowful countenance – no doubt more to himself and his friends than to Perseus: 'Why must you exonerate fate from the charge of injustice in such a miserable way? Why must you yourself give proof through your conduct that you have not met undeservedly with misfortune, that you are more worthy of your present state than of the former one?

'Why do you desecrate my victory and diminish my deeds by showing yourself to be such an ignoble and unworthy opponent? Candour and courage earn even the unfortunate man the respect of his enemies. But cowardice, even if it had good fortune on its side, has always been despised by Romans!'

Thus spoke the Roman general Lucius Aemilius Paulus. And it may be said that history has never pronounced judgement on what befits both the victor and the vanquished more clearly than through his mouth and through this scene.

5 The wife and the shoe[7]

Of the same Aemilius Paulus the following is told:

When he was about to be divorced from his wife after twenty years of marriage, his friends came to him in amazement at his plan, arguing and saying: 'She is virtuous, she is beautiful, she is fertile: what more do you want?'

Thereupon Aemilius Paulus took off his shoe and held it out to his friends with the words: 'It is dainty, it is light, it is exquisite; but do you know where it pinches me?'

---

7 This story was taken by Elias from Plutarch, *Lives*, Aemilius Paulus, v. 1–3 (Loeb edn, vol. vi, pp. 364–5).

6

Contribution to the debate on Karl Mannheim, 'The importance of competition in the intellectual field'

Dr Elias:

Ladies and gentlemen, it seems to me that we have all been affected by Dr Mannheim's paper[1] in a particular way. For precisely this reason I rather regret that this debate has not been conducted with the intensity and heat, both for and against, that the paper deserves. It has been, if I may express it in this way, a collection of monologues rather than a dialogue, a genuine confrontation of minds. Perhaps only Alfred Weber's[2] address has matched the intensity of Dr Mannheim's presentation, just because it was antagonistic in a certain way. The ideas in Dr Mannheim's paper are – and I

Translation of 'Beitrag zur Diskussion über Karl Mannheim, 'Die Bedeutung der Konkurrenz im Gebiete des Geistigen', *Verhandlungen des 6. Deutschen Soziologentages vom 17.–19.9.1928 in Zürich* (Tübingen, Mohr/Siebeck, 1929), pp. 110–11.

1 Karl Mannheim (1893–1947): Hungarian-born sociologist and founder of the sociology of knowledge. At this time, Mannheim was a *Privatdozent* (lecturer) at the University of Heidelberg. He had published numerous articles on the relationship between philosophy and sociology and on epistemology and culture. Mannheim's widely debated book *Ideology and Utopia* appeared in 1929 (trans. Edward Shils (London: Routledge & Kegan Paul, 1936)). From 1930–3 he was Professor of Sociology at the University of Frankfurt. After the Nazis came to power in 1933, Mannheim went to England, where he spent the rest of his life, researching, writing and lecturing, mainly at the London School of Economics. The focus of his work shifted towards social planning, democratic politics and education. His best-known book from his British period is *Man and Society in an Age of Reconstruction* (London: Routledge & Kegan Paul, 1940). He was appointed Professor of Education at the University of London in 1945. Mannheim's pre-1933 essays are all available in English in a number of edited collections published by Routledge between the 1950s and 1980s.

2 Alfred Weber (1868–1958), brother of Max Weber and at this time Professor of Sociology at the University of Heidelberg and Elias's *Habilitation* supervisor. Started as a political economist working on industrial location theory and later moved into culture sociology.

believe myself wholly at one with Professor Löwe[3] in this – revolutionary in a quite specific way, not in the sense of a socialist or social revolution but in that of an intellectual revolution. These ideas give expression to a fundamental breakdown of the intellectual attitude which has been predominant up to now. It appears to be the fate of Western culture that a new ideal image gradually grows up from the ideal image with which the vitality and happiness of a series of generations has been bound up. In a dialectical movement, to and fro, the new ideal attacks the older one at its core, breaks it up and finally supersedes it. What we have heard today seems to me a direct expression of such a radical switch from one quite specific type of intellectual ideal to a new and different one. And it is precisely this constellation that entitles us to speak here of a 'revolutionary' thinking which justifies the call for a more urgent response, a more passionate confrontation in our debate.

My limited time confines me to key words in speaking of the antithesis that concerns us. Allow me to sketch it very briefly. On one side is the type of truth-ideal the most striking symbols of which are not only the religious ideas of God, but the idea of the eternity of the starry heavens above us and of the moral law within us.[4] On the other side is the type of ideal which is perhaps best symbolised by the notion of the immanent regularity or necessity of an infinite flow.

Allow me, in the context of the preceding debate, to approach the antithesis at issue here from a different side. Alfred Weber made the allusion to the creative person that has already been discussed on a number of occasions. It is certainly not quite correct to claim that this idea of the creative person alone constitutes *one* side of this antithesis. But what I wish to say is not at all concerned with particular persons. What is important to me is to point out generally how the struggle between the old and new forms of consciousness is also decided in terms of one's attitude to the

3   Adolf Löwe (1893–1995), at this time Professor of Economic Theory and Sociology at the University of Kiel and one of the discussants for Mannheim's lecture. Close friend and associate of Karl Mannheim in Frankfurt 1931–3 and in England in the 1930s, when he held a post at the University of Manchester. From 1940 he taught at the New School for Social Research in New York.

4   Elias is paraphrasing here part of an often-quoted statement from Kant, which would have been very well known to his listeners. The full text in Kant is: 'Two things fill the mind with ever new and increasing admiration and awe, the oftener and more steadily we reflect on them: the starry heaven above me and the moral law within me' (Immanuel Kant, *Critique of Practical Reason*, trans. Lewis White Beck (Indianapolis and New York, Bobbs-Merrill, 1956 [orig. 1788]), p.166.)

'creative person'. The difference at issue here is one of emphasis. On one side are those who, while by no means overlooking the importance of the unextraordinary masses in all historical developments, direct all their interest and human passion not towards simple, everyday events but towards the unusual, the 'great experience', the mystery of the extraordinary. On the other side are those who believe that the mystery of the 'creative human being' is no greater than that of human beings in general. That is not to neglect or even deny the fact that one person's creative imagination is greater than another's. It is merely an expression of the awareness that the individual fate of each human being, the great and the small, is equally tied to the great, supra-individual historical fate of human societies.

This awareness is not just a theoretical affair but, to use a phrase of Alfred Weber's, an expression of a new feeling for life;[5] and if anything has affected us in Dr Mannheim's paper, it is not only the 'theory' but also precisely the human attitude, the specific 'feeling for life', that has found expression in it. Anyone who places the 'creative human being' at the centre of his reflections still has, fundamentally, the feeling of existing *for himself alone*, of himself forming, as it were, a beginning and an end. Anyone who places historical movements of human society at the centre must also know that he himself is neither beginning nor end but, if I might express it thus, a link in the chain. Clearly, this awareness imposes on its bearer a very different kind of moderation than the former viewpoint.

What all this signifies is illustrated, if you would like a single example, by a concept such as Mannheim's notion of 'consensus'. It is perhaps not without value to point out that the consensus of a given period includes far more than the examples stressed by Dr Mannheim, proverbial sayings or the knowledge that 2 times 2 equals 4. The consensus of our time also includes, for example, our specific idea of nature. Each of us, whether 'creative' or not, is *compelled* to experience events in time and space in a quite particular way that is peculiar to Western society in the modern age, namely, as 'nature'. This mode of experience is not open to decision by the individual. Whether we wish to or not, we cannot experience nature in any

5   The expression 'feeling for life' occurs in Alfred Weber's article, 'Fundamentals of culture sociology: social process, civilisational process and culture-movement', trans. G. H. Weltner and C. F. Hirshman (New York: Department of Social Science, Columbia University, 1939), p. 42. [Originally in *Archiv für Sozialwissenschaft und Sozialpolitik* 47 (1920–1): 1–49; reprinted in John Rundell and Stephen Mennell (eds), *Classical Readings in Culture and Civilisation* (London: Routledge, 1998), pp. 191–215.]

way that does not correspond to our historical situation, just as medieval people were compelled to experience nature in a quite different way to ours, as a realm of spirits. Such a consensus is the type, the scope within which the individual person, whether a genius or not, develops. Unfortunately, I must let the matter rest with such brief indications.

7

Contribution to the debate on Richard Thurnwald, 'On primitive art'

Dr Elias:

Ladies and Gentlemen: I do not intend to test your heroism much longer. Allow me to say just a few brief words. I cannot go into detail in the short time at my disposal. I should like first of all to connect today's debate with yesterday's debate. Here we have indeed one of those instances to which we must refer when we speak about 'understanding'. The question we have to consider is: have we actually *understood* the other person? Does what we have heard today help us to a better understanding of primitive people? Of course, every discipline has the right to behave as if it had already made a complete investigation of its subject matter, and to believe at any moment that it can already grasp the whole of its subject. But it is perhaps not quite without value for a critic once in a while to point out modestly what is still to be done. And I for one believe that, if one disregards scientific terminology and thinks of the living primitive man, much still needs to be done before we can really say that we have understood him. Here lies one of the most decisive problems which has to be taken into account in a theory of understanding.

The first thing we see when we encounter this strange person is that we do not understand him. In creating a theory of 'understanding', the task, therefore, is not just to show how it is possible for a human being to

Translation of 'Beitrag zur Diskussion über Richard Thurnwald, *Die Anfäng der Kunst*', *Verhandlungen des 6. Deutschen Soziologentages vom 17.–19.9.1928 in Zürich* (Tübingen, Mohr/Siebeck, 1929), pp. 281–4.

Richard Thurnwald (1869–1954), German anthropologist, known for his comparative studies of social institutions. Did fieldwork in the Solomon Islands, Micronesia, New Guinea and East Africa. Elias's contribution was the last of five in a session at the conference entitled 'Ethnological sociology: the origins of art', led by Thurnwald, who also responded to the discussants.

understand human beings, but to show at the same time how it is possible that we do *not* understand each other. And this applies of course not only to our relation to the primitive, but also, in a different form, to our relations amongst ourselves. These very debates have shown that at times we do not understand each other even amongst ourselves. So if one says that 'understanding' is based upon the fact that one mind recognises the same thing in the other, it is also necessary to explain – or at least to make intelligible – why we, who are all of the same mind, who are all people, are unable in a particular situation to understand each other.

Please do not understand by this that I am advocating a particular metaphysic, that I wish to say with all this that it is definitely impossible to understand people from another culture, that they have a nature different from ours. On the contrary, I too believe that there is only *one* 'man'. But precisely when one believes in the unity of everything human, the question of how it is possible to understand everything human, and why it is that under certain conditions one does not understand, is still more difficult and still more important. How then does science in its practice cope with this?

Allow me to tell you a small anecdote about a French army commander who was fighting a war in North Africa with native troops when, one day, there was an eclipse of the sun which caused the troops to refuse advancing further towards the enemy. He called the headman to himself and said: I shall explain to you how the eclipse of the sun comes about. Then you will see that you need to have no fear. So he explained: there is the sun, there is the earth, and there is the moon, and so on. Then, because the moon comes to stand between the earth and the sun, the eclipse of the sun comes about. Then he asked the headman whether he had understood. Yes, the headman replied, he had understood. So the general said: Right, we can proceed. 'No, we cannot', the headman retorted. 'Why not?' 'Well, it is well known', the headman answered, 'when the sun is eclipsed in this way, that is because a certain spirit holds his coat before the sun. Then one may not possibly move on.' The general shook his head and said: I have explained it to you exactly; you have not understood, and I will explain it once more. And he told the same story again, of course with the same result.

How is such non-understanding to be understood? Science, if it does not fully renounce any attempt at explaining this non-understanding, has a relatively simple way of coming to terms with this profound divergence, with this lack of a bridge between particular cultures: it describes the divergences the way one describes plants and animals, it gives them names, it says something like that the headman is entangled in magic or myth, and the European is not. But I ask you: do we as yet understand this person when we say he is tied up in *magic*? I believe that great advances have undoubtedly been made with this method – using concepts like myth, matriarchy, patriarchy. It offers a way of putting these things in some sort of order. But in dealing with something human, does all this not amount more to describing from the outside than to understanding from the inside? Regarding the possibility of understanding there are two opinions. One can say, we are definitely incapable of understanding and we must resign ourselves to that; or one can say, we are able to go much further along the road of understanding. I, too, believe that we only stand at the beginning of a real understanding of the primitive; I believe that the method followed thus far is a necessary and useful stage – but it does not yet allow us to understand the experience and forms of expression of these other, primitive people.

Allow me in this context to touch briefly upon the central question raised by the speaker, the question of the origins of art. This is certainly a very necessary and legitimate question. I believe myself to be in full agreement with the speaker, however, when I say that, just like concepts such as family, marriage and similar concepts which correspond to our own way of thinking, our concept of 'art' can self-evidently not be applied in any direct way to the creations of primitive people, simply because – and that is one of the decisive points – it implies a degree of differentiation which is not yet even present to the consciousness of the primitive people themselves. The task of understanding seems to me to be to raise the question of how the primitive himself experiences the world. Why is he *forced* to experience the world thus and not differently, and why are we *forced* – we have no choice – to experience the world thus and not differently, although both of us – probably – share the same human nature? From where does this unavoidability come, this inner necessity which makes the primitive experience a tree thus and not differently – as a spirit! – and makes it impossible for us to experience the tree as a spirit?

We who live today have not ourselves brought about the transition from a view of the world as a world of spirits to a view of the world as 'nature', but we are forced to realise in ourselves this way of experiencing the world – as an *inheritance* to which we are bound. The primitive is entirely unable to perform any of these differentiations, such as art, nature, economy and law, which we are compelled to experience as something self-evident. For in his consciousness all such differentiations, in which the world has become diversified for us, are still held together undeveloped as in an embryo. So we cannot say about the creations of primitive people that something is either a piece of art or an economic or a religious object; rather every single object belongs to all these spheres simultaneously – it contains these spheres in itself in the way the seed contains in itself undeveloped the future organs of the plant. And it is our task, in trying to understand the primitive, to detach ourselves a little from the stage of differentiation we have reached, and to place ourselves at that other point of differentiation in which all those spheres remain together undeveloped.[1]

Much more could be said. Allow me to finish by saying just one more thing. It is necessary to raise the question of why it is that the primitive is nowadays increasingly arousing our interest. I shall not go into the most interesting problem of progress raised by the speaker. Can one say that we represent progress with regard to the primitive? If all that is meant by this is the mere observation that the primitive consciousness holds undeveloped in itself that which has developed for us, one might perhaps answer this question in the affirmative; but I will not go further into that. It seems to me possible, however, to give a brief answer to the question of why the primitive arouses our interest to such an extent nowadays. In earlier times the horizon of the researcher – the philosopher as well as any other researcher into human affairs – was usually limited by the break made by the first spurt of enlightenment in antiquity;[2] today we have gradually reached the insight that the human becomes understandable only when it

1   Readers may detect in the text at this point echoes of Émile Durkheim's evolutionary theory of knowledge, in which what was culturally and institutionally fused in under conditions of mechanical solidarity gradually becomes differentiated in modern societies under organic solidarity. There is no evidence, however, that at this point in his career (1928) Elias was familiar with this aspect of Durkheim's work in any detail, although he did know the writings of his follower Lucien Lévy-Bruhl. The parallel is reinforced by Elias's evolutionary language here. Later he reserved the concept of evolution for biological systems and the concept of development for society (see Norbert Elias, *Involvement and Detachment* (Oxford: Basil Blackwell, 1987) and the revised edition in the Collected Works, vol. 8). Lévy-Bruhl (1857–1939), French philosopher, ethnographer and sociologist was associated with the group around Émile Durkheim's journal, *L'Année sociologique*. He studied in particular the contrast between Western and 'primitive' thinking. His best-known works were *How Natives Think* (1910) and *Primitive Mentality* (1923).

2   An early formulation of an idea that Elias developed in later years in a number of places as a model of successive waves of magical-mythical and secular thinking in human history. See, in particular, his *Involvement and Detachment*, part II, *The Symbol Theory* (London: Sage, 1991), pp. 132–47, and his published essays on the sociology of knowledge and science. (All of these texts will appear in later volumes in the Collected Works.)

is comprehended in its entirety. That does not precisely mean from its beginnings, for there are no absolute beginnings; but one realises that it is necessary, in order to understand *oneself*, to go back as far as at all possible in the study of man. In this sense I believe I can say that not only is every period in human history, as has been said, directly given to God, but also that – if one wishes to understand man, if one wishes to understand oneself – every period in human history is equally relevant to us.

8

The sociology of German anti-Semitism

There are two fundamentally different viewpoints regarding the phenomenon of anti-Semitism. One, that we shall call the 'enlightenment' view,
maintains that the mass of the German people is being incited against the
German Jews by certain more or less malicious or at least self-serving
people: that anti-Semitism is, as it were, 'manufactured'. According to this
view, the incitement should be countered by the most energetic possible
work of enlightenment; anti-Semitism would then be checked or even
eliminated.

The other view of anti-Semitism, the sociological one, maintains that
anti-Semitism is not 'invented' or 'concocted' by individuals and then
propagated, nor are any particular people 'to blame' for it – even though
many malicious or 'incited' people, who are capable of being 'enlightened',
may be involved in it in particular cases. The cause of anti-Semitism,
according to this view, is to be sought in the peculiar position of German
Jews, or, more precisely, of the German Jewish community, among the
various social strata of the German people. Its origins lie, it is argued, in the
specific areas of friction, in the economic, intellectual and social conflicts
of interest which exist, as a result of the social position of the Jewish
community, between its members and the members of certain other social
strata of the German people.

The peculiar rise and fall in the level of anti-Semitism in Germany
cannot be understood, according to this view, if Jewish history is inter-
preted in the normal way, that is, if the fate of the German Jews is
considered in isolation. The curve of anti-Semitism can be understood
only within the overall context of German history. Thus, one notes first of

Translation of 'The sociology of German anti-Semitism', *Israelitisches Gemeindeblatt. Offizielles
Organ der Israelitischen Gemeinden Mannheim und Ludwigshafen,* 13 Dec. 1929 (11 Kislev 5690),
7: 12, pp. 3 – 6.

all that attitudes towards the Jews are by and large the logical expression of a quite specific political view. They form part – usually not even the most important part – of the general attitude of people to the political, social and ideological questions of their time. Those in Germany who adhere to a conservative[1] view of the world are and have always been to a greater or lesser extent hostile to the Jews. The carriers of genuine liberalism and of democratic ideas are not and never have been positively hostile to the Jews, and sometimes have been more or less favourable towards them. The representatives of socialism adopt a deliberately antagonistic position towards all anti-Semitic tendencies, and earlier did so even more strongly, and the Communists likewise. Out of friendship for the Jews? Not at all. In anti-Semitism they are combating a part of a political tendency which is hostile to them in its totality.

Let us consider the constellation from which this entire development started, the period following the French Revolution. The previously domi-nant strata in Germany, the princes, the nobility and to some extent the clergy, naturally had a strong interest in maintaining the status quo of so-called 'enlightened absolutism' – the polity of estates, the authoritarian or police state. Up to the French Revolution, these groups had regarded the existing order as something self-evident, inviolable, eternal. Through the experience of the French Revolution, the preservation of the existing order and system of rule became the conscious political programme of the strata whose interests were at stake. They became 'conservative'. And their best means of publicising their view was to draw attention to the bloody deeds of the French Revolution, just as today the most effective propaganda, for all conservative groups with an interest in maintaining the established order, is to point to the actions of the Russian Revolution. At that time, however, the Jews belonged quite unambiguously to the broad middle-class mass of those who were not at all interested in preserving the existing order of estates. In their position they were even more oppressed than the Christian middle class.

As long as the medieval guild-order and its pattern of thinking prevailed – that is, in the period when the German economy was only

1 The influence of Karl Mannheim's work generally and his 1927 essay on 'Conservative thought', in particular, can be detected in this essay of Elias's. Mannheim's essay can be found in his *Essays on the Sociology and Social Psychology*, trans. and ed. Paul Kecskemeti (London: Routledge & Kegan Paul, 1953), pp. 74–164, and in *Conservatism: A Contribution to the Sociology of Knowledge*, ed. David Kettler, Volker Meja and Nico Stehr (London and New York, Routledge & Kegan Paul, 1986).

slightly affected by capitalist expansionist tendencies – there were necessarily severe tensions between the Christian town-dwellers and the Jews. In 1817, for example, the City of Frankfurt protested quite explicitly against the abolition of the medieval restrictions on Jews, pointing to the competition to which Christian traders would necessarily be exposed by being placed on an equal footing with Jewish ones. But it was in this period that the industrial, capitalist development of the German economy was gradually beginning. Such a development was possible only if all medieval restrictions on trade, and on human beings generally, were removed. The Christian middle class was coming into ever sharper conflict with all the traditional restrictions placed on people. It began to fight more and more consciously against the existing order of estates and for the free play of forces – which meant economic and political forms based on competition between free and equal individuals. In the context of this increasing expansion of the German economy, competition was no longer seen as dangerous but as fruitful and progressive, whereas any traditional restriction on freedom was now regarded as dangerous. In this situation the attitude of the Christian German middle class to the question of the emancipation of the Jews changed decisively. They now regarded the few educated Jewish merchants and bankers as welcome allies in building up the German economy. In opposing the traditional legislation concerning the Jews, the liberal Christian middle class was now combating a part of the traditional restriction on freedom; it was opposing the order of estates itself. Emancipation appeared to it as the first prerequisite for the education of the Jewish masses as good, hard-working German citizens. We can see quite clearly here how the attitude to the Jews was a function of general social attitudes and the corresponding perceptual field. The liberal merchant necessarily saw in the Jew something quite different from what was perceived by the conservative noble landowner. That the conservative elements of that time were against the emancipation of the Jews was not the result of malice or 'incitement', but a special case of the general conservative attitude of opposition to any change in the existing social order of estates and the corresponding structure of rule.

Similarly, the support of all the liberal elements of that time for the emancipation of the Jews was not the expression of any special fondness of the Christian middle class for the Jews, but a necessary consequence of the specific social situation and objectives of this liberal bourgeoisie. There are examples of influential leaders of the liberal movement who, shortly after being involved in angry personal clashes with Jewish bankers, supported Jewish emancipation in parliament. Thus, the likelihood that bad personal experiences with individual Jews will be generalised into an 'anti-Semitic mentality' varies under different social and therefore different ideological circumstances.

I shall turn now from that initial constellation to the present one. A number of factors are crucial for an understanding of the change in the position of the German Jews which has occurred since that time. First, the about-face of the German middle class which has taken place in the last century. A hundred years ago, for the reasons just sketched, the battlefront of the middle class faced primarily towards the right, against the ruling stratum of the nobility and the existing absolutist order of estates. At that time the German middle class was anything but conservative. It was genuinely 'liberal' and in part democratic. That struggle between the middle class and the nobility is now finally over. Politically, the nobility no longer has any special rights. In terms of economic power, and therefore of real power in the state, it has fallen far behind the bourgeoisie. The middle class has triumphed. It has itself become socially, economically and politically the ruling stratum; its battlefront no longer faces right, but left, against the newly rising stratum of the proletariat. And just as earlier the nobility sought to defend the existing order and its own dominance against the rising middle class, today the middle class is defending the existing order against the following stratum. It has itself become the stratum that seeks to 'conserve'. The opposition between conservatism and liberalism has been largely abolished. As was made explicit, for example, in Mahraum's manifesto,[2] the ideology of the middle class represents, with varying nuances, a synthesis of conservative, liberal and, to an extent, democratic ideas.

The position of the German-Jewish community within this social movement was a very peculiar one. Economically, their position was, roughly speaking, the same as that of the middle-class Christian community. The Jewish community, too, had its battle front largely facing left, as protector of the existing economic order against the new stratum of the rising proletariat. Socially, however, it was not on an equal footing with good middle-class Christian society, but was regarded by the latter as something like a second rank middle class. This difference between its economic position within the camp of the dominant middle class confronting the

2 Artur Mahraum, *Das jungdeutsche Manifest: Volk gegen Kaste und Geld* (Berlin: Jungdeutscher Verlag, 1927).

advancing working class, and its social position as a second-rank middle class, forced it in the same direction as the working class in disapproving or even combating the existing social order in some form. This difference was the source of many conflicts, and it also contributed to the peculiar agitation and loss of cohesion in the lives of many Jews that are familiar to us.

How is this evaluation as a second-rank community to be explained? There are various reasons, but only two of the most important ones will concern us here. First, there were undeniable inward and outward differences between the majority of German Jews and the majority of German Christians, whether one prefers to explain them more by descent or more by upbringing, or by both – that is, by the totality of their historical and social fate. Although these differences certainly were not in themselves the reason for the 'second-rank' status, they could give rise to such an evaluation in a situation of conflict. In fact, the otherness of the Jews only became a topical and relevant concern for the Christian middle class, both as a reality and as an argument in the social struggle, within very specific constellations. In the years of the first great expansion of capitalist tendencies in Germany, this otherness did not give the middle class any grounds for hostile arguments. Competition from the Jews may sometimes have made itself felt among small shopkeepers, but certainly was not especially noticeable in the leading strata of the German middle class. In this period, which was discussed earlier, Jews – and there were never very many of them who came into consideration – were admitted to the student fraternities. From that time on, however, the curve of anti-Semitism rose gradually, and the crests of its wave motion always coincided with times when the economic situation was tense and when conflicts of interest and, above all, competition – which naturally, in the first instance, was competition from those who were different – were especially keenly felt. This development cannot be discussed in detail here. As an example, the present situation is enough.

As a result of losing the war, economic space for all Germans has become extraordinarily constricted. But it has not been restricted for all strata of the German people to the same extent. It can be shown quite clearly that anti-Semitism is strongest in those middle-class strata whose economic space, compared to the time before and during the war, has been constricted the most. To characterise the present phase of social development, it can be said of specific strata that if they are not actually in the process of disintegration, they are clearly in steep decline. They include, above all, the formerly independent small businesses and also, in part, large businesses. In addition, though only in some sectors, they include medium-sized manufacturing industry, which is being forced increasingly into dependency. In many regions the situation of farmers and of some large landowners, though different in other ways, is similar in being unfavourable. It is precisely these strata, and particularly their young people, who form the backbone of the National Socialist movement. For them the distinctiveness, the otherness of the Jews is what lays them open to attack. If one adds that in the post-war period Jews have emerged more prominently than before in leading positions in the state, and in some cases as leaders of the working class, one has at least an initial overview of the structure of the prevailing wave of anti-Semitism. The farmer knows the Jew above all in the social guise of the livestock dealer or small trader, while the town-dwellers and large landowners know him more particularly in that of the banker, the finance minister (for example, National Socialism's fight against 'interest slavery'[3]). For all these groups, mortgages, taxes and bank debts are the most oppressive, most abstract of burdens. To give just a few more examples, the small trader also knows the Jew, if not directly as a competitor, at least in the form of the department store owner. Other hard-pressed groups, the *Lumpenproletariat*, the unemployed, agricultural labourers, are swept along by the simple slogans directed against strangers. It is among these groups, some moribund and some at least severely constricted, that the crudest form of anti-Semitism has taken root. But tensions which manifest themselves in hostility to the Jews also exist between heavy industry and finance capital,[4] while there is also competition between the Christian and Jewish lawyer or doctor. It is not possible to go into detail here. It is enough to point out what is fundamentally important: that the now conservative Christian German middle class faces a struggle of greater or lesser severity in Germany's restricted economic space. In the

---

3 'Interest slavery' – a phrase coined in 1919 by the National Socialist ideologue Gottfried Feder (1883–1941). Hitler used it in *Mein Kampf*, referring to Feder, when describing what he saw as the debt bondage imposed on everyone by Jewish-dominated, international finance capital. The abolition of 'interest slavery' formed an important part of the radical, anti-capitalist aspect of the emerging ideology of the National Socialists. The 'Jewish question' was thus implicated in their political programme from the outset. See Elias's later analysis of the role of National Socialist beliefs in his *The Germans: Power Struggles and the Development of Habitus in the Nineteenth and Twentieth Centuries*, ed. Michael Schröter, trans. Eric Dunning and Stephen Mennell (Cambridge: Polity, 1996, part IV (Collected Works, vol. 11)).

4 Cf. Ludwig Bernhard, *Der Hugenbergkonzern* (Berlin: J. Springer, 1928), pp. 27ff (N.E.).

form of anti-Semitism it is fighting against those of its competitors and bourgeois opponents of its own interests who seem easiest to strike against and render harmless. These are the members of a special and always more or less conspicuous group, a group which, moreover, because of its second-rank status, always displays certain tendencies which 'undermine' the existing order. Depending on the social situation, the middle class fights them now with crude, now with more sophisticated means, using now this, now that ideological superstructure. It is conducting this struggle as a conflict of social interests and world-views, in exactly the same way as it is waging a struggle against the rising stratum of the proletariat.

So much for the diagnosis. It is not possible in this context to talk of a treatment; or, more precisely, it follows from this diagnosis that no treatment, no definitive remedy for the sickness of anti-Semitism in the social body, exists in the present state of society. The wave-like movement of anti-Semitism is a function of an economic and social development which cannot be changed, and can scarcely be influenced in any way, by the small group of German Jews. In this respect the Jewish community is far more driven than driving. From this realisation, in conjunction with other experiences, one may draw the conclusion that a social order in which a group of gifted, often spiritually and intellectually rich and productive people is deliberately degraded and debased, and thus is violently crippled, does not deserve to exist and must be fought. One may conclude that it is necessary to emigrate to Palestine, since the struggle for a national homeland for the Jews seems more fruitful than the struggle for social equality for the Jews in Germany. All that is left for those who do not wish to draw such conclusions is resignation. In any case, a clear understanding of one's own position is better than desolate self-deception. Only one thing is still possible for German Jews in response to anti-Semitism: to accustom themselves to the unobtrusive but resolute and self-confident demeanour which alone befits their situation.

9

The kitsch style and the age of kitsch

In memory of Wolfgang Hellmert [1]

I

That bourgeois strata fought their way to supremacy in the West in the course of the nineteenth century is well known; and the importance of bourgeois dominance for the social and political fate of nations has been discussed and evaluated often enough.

The profound transformation of aesthetic forms which took place in this period – the changes in architectural style or clothing, for example – has also been frequently mentioned and described.

But the connection between these two sets of changes, in society and aesthetics, has hardly ever been thoroughly investigated or made visible. One feels that there is a deeper division between the styles of the eighteenth and nineteenth centuries than between what we call the baroque and the rococo. But this difference in the nature of the aesthetic change only becomes clear if it is understood in terms of the situation of the society concerned. The change from the 'baroque' to the 'rococo', from

Translation of 'Kitschstil und Kitschzeitalter', *Die Sammlung: Literarische Monatsschrift unter dem Patronat von André Gide, Aldous Huxley, Heinrich Mann*, ed. Klaus Mann, 2: 5 (Amsterdam, 1935): 252–63.

1 Wolfgang Hellmert (1906–34), German poet, part of Klaus Mann's circle in Paris in the early 1930s. He committed suicide in May 1934. In his autobiography, *The Turning Point: Thirty-Five Years in this Century: The Autobiography of Klaus Mann* (New York: Markus Wiener, 1984), Mann describes his friend Wolfgang Hellmert as 'bland and civilised' (p. 288) and recalls other friends who also committed suicide in the 1930s. Mann poignantly mentions that as the theme for the last story he wrote before his suicide, Hellmert chose a line from Hölderlin: 'Leicht zerstörbar sind die Zärtlichen' ('Easily destructible are the tender ones'). Klaus Mann himself committed suicide in 1949.

the 'Louis Quatorze' to the 'Régence'[2] style, is a change within the framework of the *same* social stratum. The deeper division which exists between the characteristic forms of the eighteenth and nineteenth centuries is an expression of the rise to power of a new social stratum, the capitalist-industrial bourgeoisie. Court style and taste were replaced by those of the capitalist bourgeoisie.

It has sometimes been said that the eighteenth century was the last to have a 'style' at all. And indeed, hardly has one dared to entertain the idea of a capitalist style than the doubts set in: Can one still speak of a 'style' in this context? It seems clear that the rise of bourgeois professional and industrial society was marked not only by the replacement of one aesthetic, one 'style' by another, but by the collapse of a coherent set of typical expressive forms. The aesthetic productions of capitalist society therefore tend to be described, far more than earlier ones, in relation to the single creative individual, or at most to various schools and tendencies. The existence of a unified development of forms and of common, typical basic structures, in short, of a 'style' of art works in the capitalist world, remains more or less obscure. Names have been found, at most, for episodes in this development, for example, the so-called Jugendstil.[3] A more comprehensive name is lacking, and the problem itself has hardly yet emerged into our consciousness.

If the term 'kitsch style' is used here to fill this gap, that may seem like a piece of eccentricity or even a malicious depreciation of the art of our time. In reality, the choice of this term is anything but a tendentious whim. For if we look beyond the general terms 'capitalist' or 'liberal' for underlying concepts expressing what is uniform in capitalist aesthetic idiom, after much sifting of words which are either colourless or imply a positive evaluation, one comes across this term as one of the very few which express a pervasive feature of capitalist aesthetic products. To be sure, the term 'kitsch' is unclear enough in common usage. But if it can and should mean anything more than a random hotchpotch of tasteless abominations, if it is to be condensed from its vague generality to embrace the concrete phenomenon which underlies its topicality in our day, then its content and boundaries must be sought in the evolution of aesthetic form within

2 Régence – style associated with the period of the French Regency, 1715–23.

3 Jugendstil – German version of Art Nouveau, the intricate, decorative art style associated with Gustav Klimt in Germany and William Morris and Aubrey Beardsley in Britain in the late nineteenth and early twentieth centuries.

bourgeois society. That the peculiarity of an age first becomes visible from a negative aspect is certainly not without precedent in history. Originally, terms such as 'baroque' or 'gothic' did not have a much more positive ring than 'kitsch' has today. Their value-content changed only in the course of social development, and – without giving undue weight to historical parallels – the term 'kitsch style' is introduced here with the same likelihood and expectation that its value may change, and to help prepare for such a change. It is used, first of all, to designate the stylistic character of the pre-war period. But no one is able to say whether we ourselves are not still 'pre-war' – that is, more closely tied to the pre-1914 period, when seen in a historical perspective than appears to us today from our close, foreshortening viewpoint.

What the term 'kitsch style' is intended to express first of all is an aesthetic quality of a very peculiar kind, namely the greater formal uncertainty inherent in all artistic production within industrial society. This can already be seen in the very early stages of the bourgeois-capitalist era. For to begin with, liberal-bourgeois society certainly did not express itself in entirely new forms. Ornamentation persisted, and *Empire*[4] and *Biedermeier*[5] were clearly descendants of the old court style. What was lost, above all, was the certainty of taste and of the creative imagination, the solidity of the formal tradition which was discernible earlier in even the clumsiest products. Outbursts of feeling of unprecedented intensity shattered the old forms; groping for new ones, artists produced some well-formed works but, to an unprecedented degree, others marked by an extreme want of clarity and taste. In this groping, this coexistence of high standards with a total lack of standards, not only in different artists but often in one and the same individual, the changed structure of the artistic process found especially vivid expression. For even the most capable artist, the lapse into formlessness now became an acute and constant threat. Every successful, fully formed work was now wrested from the abyss to a quite different extent than had been the case earlier, when a firm social tradition both fettered and sustained the creative urge. The formal tendencies of the works of great artists, whether they were called Heine or

4 Empire style – neo-classical ornamental style in the decorative arts prevalent in France in the first part of the nineteenth century, named after the 'First Empire' of Napoleon I, 1804–15.

5 Biedermeier – German style of furniture, decoration and art of the early to mid-nineteenth century modelled on the French 'Empire' style.

Victor Hugo, Wagner or Verdi, Rodin or Rilke, were intimately connected to those displayed by the mediocre works, which we dismiss as aberrations, as products of disintegration and decadence, as 'kitsch'; one merges easily and imperceptibly into the other. Kitsch in the negative sense, therefore, is never only something antagonistic, existing outside the works of the true creators, but is also a basic situation within them, a part of themselves. This incessant interpenetration of structure and disintegration is a feature of the enduring regularity to be observed in industrial society. It could be demonstrated no less in the works of the nineteenth than of the twentieth century in the West, in Balzac as in Gide, in Ingres as in Picasso. And it is felt most strongly in precisely those works of this era in which form is most highly developed. The powerful accentuation, the peculiarly artificial and sometimes almost convulsive intensity of form characteristic of some of the greatest modern artists, expresses, fundamentally, nothing other than this insecurity, this unremitting struggle against formlessness and disintegration which even the most accomplished artists have to wage today. Think of Stefan George or Paul Valéry, of Proust or Thomas Mann, whose urbanely ironic speech rhythm is nothing but a rampart of this kind. So much has dilapidation become in our age a constitutive element, decisively affecting even the positive aspect of artistic works. And, as can be seen, the re-evaluation of kitsch as a positive concept began already in that period.

II

There were gifted artists who created their works between the firm river banks of a strong formal tradition, supported and restrained by the bearer of this tradition, a non-capitalist 'good society'. They were followed by others who had to make their way without such support, relying far more on themselves. But, certainly, the boundary-line between the two types can be only approximately drawn. Outwardly, the transition between them is made most strikingly visible by the destruction of the Parisian court society in the French Revolution. But this event was only a symptom of a comprehensive social re-grouping which took place very gradually. Even the *pre*-revolutionary Greuze and the *pre*-revolutionary David were representatives of the new bourgeois style and belonged, to an extent, to the age of kitsch. Between them on one side and the representatives of the court idiom, Watteau, Fragonard and Boucher on the other, art slowly changed its direction.

The same is true of literature. In this area, too, at somewhat different times in each country, depending on its stage of social development, the same turning point is discernible. In France it is to be found roughly between Voltaire and Balzac, in Germany between Goethe and Heine. But even Goethe and Voltaire were no longer *ancien régime* in the strict sense, but more or less transitional figures on the periphery of court society.

Voltaire's style and sense of form were schooled and polished directly within the circles of the court nobility. Throughout his life he remained strongly attached to the traditions of this society with regard to form and taste. His deep understanding, his assurance in matters of form and taste were entirely of that society. But that he, the son of bourgeois parents, turned partly against the conservative maxims of court circles where reason and religion were concerned, that he *was able* to turn against them, already expresses the transitional situation of that society. He was exposed to the influences both of the high court society, which was already very decentralised, and of the bourgeois capitalist one which was gradually coming into being and emancipating itself.

In a different sense, corresponding to the different structure of the German countries, Goethe, too, was such a marginal figure, on the periphery of the court era and facing towards the bourgeois age. However, we should never forget that the *ancien régime* survived in Prussia-Germany, in a bourgeoisified and industrial form, until 1918, whereas it had by and large been demolished in France in 1789. But in France, with its continuous tradition over many centuries, the form-creating power of court society was extraordinarily strong. Despite its eradication as a political system, therefore, the *ancien régime*, through its tradition with regard to taste, has continued to exert, in that country, a vigorous influence within the framework of the industrial age and the kitsch style, until the present. In the most influential German country, Prussia, by contrast, the form-creating, cultural strength of court society, and thus the weight exerted on the kitsch style by the court tradition, was less. The uncertainty of taste was consequently greater, but so, too, was the willingness to try out new forms and directions.

Moreover, in this Germany of petty courts, the true culture-creating or at least culture-consuming stratum was formed, not by a nobility living on unearned income, but by a special form of the middle and upper civil service, which hardly existed in France and which included clergymen and university teachers no less than officers, court officials and the administrators of large estates. While this German bureaucracy, largely drawn from the bourgeoisie, always lived in a special dependence on court society proper, in secret it generally harboured a hopeless, almost unrealisable opposition to the court system, at least as long as it was largely denied access to the highest positions within court and government. German literature, from Lessing through the *Sturm und Drang*[6] and the period of 'Sentimentalism' up to the Romanticism of the nineteenth and twentieth centuries, is full of testimonies to this impotent protest. And Goethe, too, must be understood within this context.

To be sure, Goethe belonged to the relatively small group of those who succeeded in rising from the bourgeoisie to the top of an official hierarchy and a court society. For this reason, too, he long remained a model and a wishful image for the German middle classes. He assimilated the attitudes and manners of court circles, but these were loose enough to allow him to manage and develop the court heritage in a highly independent way. In this fruitful situation of transition, the social bonds still offered the individual the firm support of a tradition while leaving him much personal latitude. It is not least this situation which allows the direction in which Goethe's mighty talent expressed itself to be understood. He developed a greatness which was strictly bound to classicist forms, but at the same time had a very personal and individual coloration.

Of course, just like Voltaire or – in the field of music – Mozart[7] (admittedly, a less marginal figure and a more direct representative of the *ancien régime*), he wrote works of very variable stature, shaped with greater or lesser power. But they are never formless; these men never ceased being guided by the accustomed good taste, which was demanded and monitored by society; their individual feeling never ruptured and destroyed the prescribed formal idiom. In this they differ fundamentally from the artists of the age of kitsch. They widened the traditional elements of style and expression, and indeed felt a lessening of their pressure. But in the end they managed all this within the framework of the prevailing stylistic convention.

---

6 *Sturm und Drang* (Storm and Stress) – the period in German literature between about 1770 and 1784 known for its accent on nature, subjectivity and youthful rebellion. Includes the famous figures of Goethe, Lessing, Herder and Schiller. Elias's familiarity with Goethe's conception of nature is clear from section IX of Elias's essay 'On seeing in nature' of 1921, pp. 5–21 above.

7 Elias returned to Mozart in a later work. See his *Mozart: Portrait of a Genius*, ed. Michael Schröter (Cambridge: Polity, 1993), Collected Works, vol. 12.

How much this changed in the following generations is well known. Beethoven, in whose hands the traditional formal and expressive idiom began to break up, was a far more marginal and transitional figure than Mozart or even Goethe. His inborn talent actually benefited from the fertility of the transitional situation. Later, however, in the succeeding generations, the break was complete. Here, in Schubert or Schumann, Heine or Balzac – to pick out a few of the many names – the sure guidance was lost. Side-by-side with highly successful works, fully formed in a comparatively individual way, we find uncontrolled outbursts of feeling, aberrations and lapses of taste. The kitsch style, with its specifically new greatness and smallness, has arrived.

III

In the nineteenth century good taste was upheld by a different social stratum from previously. The position of the artist and the social function of art changed radically in bourgeois-industrial society. As the bourgeois influence spread through the whole of society, what had previously been handed down tacitly and almost automatically within the medium of the more stable 'good society' – *savoir vivre*, the correct attitude, assured taste – ceased to be imparted imperceptibly to each member of the social group concerned, and had to be taught to individuals by specialists. Napoleon consciously schooled himself, using actors as models. The dandy Beau Brummell, the archetypal specialist in taste, had to instruct English good society, the courtiers and even the Prince Regent himself, in poise and taste. An especially impressive example of this change is to be found in the history of painting. Up to Manet and the Impressionists, it had been 'good societies', ruling social groups, which had set their stamp – if to an ever-diminishing extent – on the prevailing style of painting as an important means of social representation. But with the Impressionists, for the first time, a specialist art asserted itself very clearly against the predominant social art and the prevailing taste. And from then on, the peculiarity of great art and the situation experienced by its creators cannot be fully under-stood unless this specialised individualisation – the growing self-reliance of artists, the total change in their position within society – is seen constantly permeating the changing forms of their works and the figures depicted. The Impressionists were thoroughly bourgeois people and by no means revolutionaries in the social sense, or clear representatives of a class rising from below to challenge the ruling bourgeoisie. This working society's incomprehension of their art is symptomatic not of the social tension between different strata of workers, but rather of the rift and tension between the taste of the leading specialists in great art of every kind on one side, and of the mass society of non-specialists, on the other.

Poussin and Watteau, Racine and even Voltaire, produced their works as servants, or at least as social inferiors, primarily for a court society which played an active part in shaping artistic taste. While Goethe rose to a position of equality, he was always contained and controlled by a rigid, socially powerful group. Manet, Cézanne and Picasso, by contrast, or Valéry and George, were all roughly the social equals of their clientèle. But by that time, as isolated individuals in the free market, using their own resources or with the support of patrons, they had to offer their wares to a more or less unknown public. Small groups of connoisseurs and collectors, who were also specialists, found themselves and their lives expressed and heightened in this art. Around them a small coterie of snobs and imitators pretended to respond to it, since that at least conferred prestige. Beyond them the bulk of society stood puzzled and uncomprehending before these works which they were unable to see as representing, at least indirectly, their own psychic condition.

The term 'kitsch' is nothing other than an expression for this tension between the highly formed taste of the specialists and the undeveloped, unsure taste of mass society. The word 'kitsch' probably originated in a specialist milieu of artists and art dealers in Munich in the early twentieth century, being first used to refer to certain 'sketches' which sold well among American tourists. The word 'kitsch' was thus derived from 'sketch'. Anything intended to be sold was said to be made for *Verkitschen*, for turning into kitsch. In this original meaning of the term 'kitsch', the whole contempt of the specialist for the uneducated taste of capitalist society is expressed, as well as the tragic aspect of this constellation, in which the specialists, whether artists, dealers or publishers, were obliged for economic reasons, to produce and sell products which they themselves despised.

The public, with all the economic and social power it wielded, necessarily had an impact on the specialists and their taste. And slowly, and often with a long time-lag, the specialists also influenced the development of public taste. Despite all the tensions between the two, this interdependence gave rise to a certain linkage of expressive forms, as when the specialist forms of 'Expressionism' or 'Cubism' were adopted, after a time and in modified form, in advertising posters or coffee-house architecture. But in addition, the two poles between which the kitsch style emerged, specialist taste and the taste of the multi-strata mass society, were linked by their common experiences and situation, the great destiny which swept all factions along together like an uncontrollable river – a destiny symbolised by wars or social conflicts, prosperity or crises. This encompassing regularity finally endowed the expressive forms of the fragmented society with a very specific uniformity, a 'style' which, admittedly, in keeping with the structure of the underlying society, was looser, more disparate and richer in contrasts than earlier styles.

IV

The particular formal problems raised by the kitsch style – which are highly revealing with regard to the lives of our fathers, and our own – still need to be resolved. In this context I must be content with a few pointers which at least show where the problems are to be found.

1   Leisure dreams of a working society[8]

If we leave aside obviously utilitarian forms, any aesthetic work has for the 'public', for the mass of the working population, the function of a leisure dream. This function gives our arts a very different face, compared to those of court, patrician or church hierarchies. The need of mass society for leisure pastimes, which the specialists have to satisfy, is supplementary to the primary needs for work and bread. It is never as vitally important as these, and the form it takes is determined by them – for example, by the constant strain of working life, the desire to discharge feelings heavily suppressed in that life, or the tendency to seek in leisure substitute satisfactions for wishes not fulfilled by work. In face of the compulsive way in which working life pushes the leisure activities of industrial man in a highly specific direction, the individual art specialist is powerless. He may poke fun at such activities as much as he likes, deriding as 'kitsch' the

8 This section on work and leisure contains adumbrations of ideas and problems which Elias pursued in greater depth in later research. See Norbert Elias and Eric Dunning, *Quest for Excitement: Sport and Leisure in the Civilising Process* (Oxford: Basil Blackwell, 1986), Collected Works, vol. 7.

leisure dreams and the taste of souls deformed by work pressures, and mocking the 'sentimental' manner in which feelings pent up and damaged under the constraint of work are expressed. *The need for what is here called 'kitsch' is socially imposed*, while kitsch itself, in the negative sense of the word, is a faithful reflection of a psychic condition engendered by industrial society. This endows the problem of kitsch with a seriousness with which it is not normally credited.

2   The emancipation of individual feeling

Almost all of the mediocre products of the kitsch era, and very many of the great ones, are distinguished from those of the past by a specific and especially powerful emotional charge. This manifests itself in the great works of music, for example, in which, from Beethoven, Schubert and Schumann, and high points such as Verdi and Wagner, to Debussy, Ravel, Stravinsky and Weill, the permeation by feeling is carried forward through ever-new forms to ever-new strata of society. In painting, too – again disregarding certain contrary tendencies – this phenomenon is no less clearly discernible. From at least the Impressionists onwards, despite the assertions of many artists themselves, what is presented again and again, and far more strongly than ever before, is not the so-called objective world but nature with its particular emotive value, as experienced and felt by the individual. This emotive charge manifests itself no less forcibly in what is called 'kitsch' in the negative sense, in kitsch postcards, for example, which are designed solely to touch the beholder's feelings, or in sentimental popular songs. It is characteristic of the problems posed by kitsch that the form of expression used in such songs seems so false and almost ridiculous, whereas the emotional need behind them, born of the impossibility of finding in scanty leisure time the relationships which working life precludes, is absolutely genuine.

3   Progressive and conservative tendencies of the kitsch style

In industrial societies the disputes over the proper modes of expression of human life are hardly carried on any longer between the various social strata themselves, but between art specialists who act, consciously or unconsciously, as representatives of particular social groups and tendencies. Hence, peculiar tensions are to be found in the aesthetic sphere of industrial society which correspond fairly exactly to the existing social tensions. One pole is formed by tendencies which consciously or unconsciously take the artistic styles of earlier societies as their models. Its representatives are willing to admit only the great and the sublime, that is, an idealised and heavily censored version of existence, into the sanctuary of art. The other pole is formed by tendencies seeking to explode existing artistic forms and to find new forms for the new human and social situation, the changed relationships and experiences characteristic of industrial society. The former seek refuge from the uncertainty pressing in on them in the idealised world of beautiful forms. But whereas, for their models, this world was made available to a high degree by the secure sense of form and the firmly established style of the society around them, their later emulators have to struggle to recreate it over and over again as isolated individuals.

The artists representing the other, progressive pole, such as Zola or Malraux, the early Gerhard Hauptmann or Brecht, want to wrest certain experiences from the mechanism of concealment. They no longer want to hide pettiness and confusion, shabbiness and helplessness behind the symmetry of well-rounded forms; in addition to joy and a masterful bearing they also seek means of expressing threat, dirt and danger, deformity and excess. The problems inherent in their work are certainly different, but no less serious, than those facing the conservative artists. In the works of the latter, to put it briefly, a form which is at least still half-traditional too readily overwhelms the content; it excludes certain experiences, ideas and situations. The danger for the progressive artists is the converse, the overwhelming of form by content. For in their work it is on content, on the idea and what is to be represented, that the primary accent is placed.

In this antithesis, however, the social tension is exactly reflected. Within a given ruling class, as it distances itself from the stratum below it, attitude and gesture, ostentation and the 'how' of representation, have always been of special importance. They are instruments of distancing. For the new, rising groups, by contrast, idea and content, precisely what the conservative classes would like to censor and leave unsaid, are incomparably more important than form. This helps to explain the preponderant role played by content and subject matter, whether it be feeling or purpose, in the art works of the kitsch era – in all the inferior works and in many of the successful ones – as compared to the *form* of representation. It results not least from the characteristic constellation which makes it relatively easy to rise from the strata of the masses, but more and more difficult for a 'good society' to encapsulate and consolidate itself, to maintain a rigid tradition of social forms. Restlessness increases, families rise and fall more rapidly, there is a relative atomisation of society and aesthetic influence passes gradually from fixed social circles to isolated taste-specialists and their schools. In conjunction with technological change and other factors which cannot be considered here, all this causes the mechanism of aesthetic production to operate very differently in industrial society than in those which preceded it. For this reason the chasm between the kitsch style and earlier styles is particularly deep.

The term 'kitsch' tends towards vagueness. I leave the argument about definitions to others. What have concerned me here are the conditions which gave rise, not to the term, but to 'kitsch' and the kitsch style itself. Did kitsch also exist at earlier times? That remains to be investigated. It will undoubtedly have existed if similar conditions of production were present earlier. Otherwise, to refer to earlier formal qualities as 'kitsch' is no more than an empty analogy. Whether the paradoxical and antinomic connection between the great works of the artist-specialists and the works produced to satisfy mass taste is seen today depends on the visual perceptiveness of the individual. The term 'kitsch style' has been used here to point to this connection. The difficult fecundity, the problematic greatness of our social and artistic existence are encompassed by this term. But so, too, are the awareness of the radical transformation in which we are involved, and a presentiment of the immense new artistic possibilities which lie before us on the journey on which we have embarked.

10

The expulsion of the Huguenots from France

Towards the end of the sixteenth century, the Protestants in France had been more or less assured of equal rights with the Catholics by the famous Edict of Nantes. In the penultimate decade of the seventeenth century these rights were taken from them and the majority of Protestants were expelled from France.

Why? What had happened?

When he came to the throne, Louis XIV had expressly confirmed to the Huguenots – or to the adherents of the RPR, the *Religion Prétendue Réformée*, as they were officially called – freedom of worship and all the rights they had been granted under the Edict of Nantes. This certainly did not put an end to the tensions between French Catholics and Protestants. But these tensions became a threat only to the weaker party when poverty increased in France.

The Protestants may not have been economically weaker than the Catholics. On the contrary, the wealth-owning strata in France, the great French merchants and financiers, were mainly Protestant, whereas very few of the noble families who had converted to Protestantism during the religious wars remained true to the reformed faith. But taken as a whole, the Protestants did constitute only a minority. Those making up, above all, the administration, the judiciary and the army, the whole apparatus of royal rule were, leaving aside a few exceptions, Catholics. In practice, access to the bureaucracy and the court – the chief means of advancement in this society – was difficult for Protestants. For just this reason their

Translation of 'Die Vertreibung der Hugenotten aus Frankreich', *Der Ausweg, Zeitschrift für Umschichtung Wanderung Siedlung* 1:12 (Paris, Oct. 1935): 369–76. The original German article, published in 1935, is attributed to 'Dr. Norbert Elias, Cambridge'. According to his *Reflections on a Life* (Cambridge: Polity, 1994), p. 49, Elias left France for England in 1935. This suggests that although the article was written and published in Paris, by the time it appeared Elias was already in England.

energies were constantly channelled into activities in commerce, industry and finance. These provided a new opportunity for advancement, the only one left open to them by the ruling Catholic society.

A French historian sums up this situation as follows: 'Persecution engendered in the Huguenots the very capacity to enrich themselves for which the descendants of their persecutors censure them today. By the seventeenth century the jealousy of the poor for the rich, of the petty trader for the great merchant, of the weak industrialist for the strong one, of land for money, can be seen contributing to the hatred of Catholics for Protestants.'[1]

That the Catholic clergy fought with all their might against the emergence of another church hierarchy alongside their own could be taken for granted. And Louis XIV, who was accustomed to looking on France as a head of a household looks on his house – that is, as a piece of property subject to his sole will – Louis XIV took it as a personal affront that some of his subjects rejected the religion which he held to be right. He wished, and stated this wish often enough, that within the unified kingdom everyone should profess the same religion – *his* own. It is no accident, however, that he became seriously preoccupied with the question of the Protestants only decades after his accession to power. We can understand fairly readily when and why this became a critical issue. It was at the time when France's external expansion was meeting with ever greater difficulties, while social pressures within the country were increasing.

At that time France was the most densely populated country in Europe. What in Germany are called 'Louis XIV's predatory wars' were to a very substantial extent the consequence of the pressure which everywhere appears to be exerted, under certain circumstances, by more densely populated regions on less densely populated ones. This pressure is less detectable at times of economic prosperity, but it grows, it strains towards relief, it becomes what we are in the habit of calling 'overpopulation', when the bulk of the population finds it harder and harder to meet their basic needs. There are a number of ways in which relief can be obtained for such relative overpopulation – relative, that is, in respect to a particular economic and political system, since, measured by its current population density, France at the time of Louis XIV was by no means a heavily populated country. One form of release is war, another is peaceful emigration, a

1 Ernest Lavisse, *Louis XIV: La Fronde, Le roi, Colbert (1643–85)*, vol. VII, part 1 of Lavisse (ed.), *Histoire de France depuis les origines jusqu'à la révolution* (Paris: Hachette, 1905), p. 41.

third is the more or less forcible expulsion of certain population groups, while a fourth is revolution, a violent change of the existing system of rule and economic organisation.

Louis XIV's expansionist wars, initially successful, ended only by increasing the level of poverty in France. They exhausted the country. In his own consciousness, the king was driven by the desire to increase his own power and fame, by the wish to be the greatest ruler in Europe; but in fact he was driven also by the need for conspicuous outward successes in order to justify, and reduce to a somewhat bearable level, the pressure of the immense burden which he and his governmental apparatus imposed on his subjects. Initially, the specific economic development of his country provided him with the necessary instruments. While it impoverished the rural masses, it favoured certain intermediate strata of the urban, commercial population. And while the former flocked to join the army, the wealth of the middle class flowed, forcibly, into the king's coffers. Voluntary and involuntary contributions, a level of taxation which accounted for 35 per cent – or, according to Taine's[2] estimate, as much as 50 per cent – of the income of the taxable strata, financed the wars. Population growth also benefited the army. Between 1672 and 1678 the number of regular troops rose from 180,000 to 400,000.

Within this overall development, the Treaties of Nijmegen in 1678–9 formed a kind of turning point. They brought many benefits. They made the king appear to be, indeed, the mightiest ruler in Europe. But, measured by the dreams and wishes of the king and the needs of the country, they brought very little. While, in the short term, the outward glory of France was enhanced, in the long term the Treaties brought inward poverty. Holland, the main adversary, was not defeated, still less overrun and destroyed. And yet the king had thought it best to lay down his arms. The trade agreement demanded by the Dutch was more favourable to them than to France. Louis XIV had come up against the limits of his power. The internal pressure in the country had not been alleviated by the military success; poverty and tensions had only been increased. And at such a moment, when the external foe, despite all the apparent successes, has put

2 Probably a reference to data cited in one of the works of the French historian Hippolyte Taine (1828–93), although in which of his texts Elias does not say. Elias had already quoted Taine's *Les Origines de la France contemporaine*, 3 vols (Paris: Hachette, 1878–92), albeit on a different topic, in his *Habilitation* dissertation on the court society, completed two years before this article was written. See *The Court Society*, Collected Works, vol. 2.

up stronger resistance than had been expected, there is an increasing inclination to seek and find the enemy within the country itself. Rulers and peoples seldom take upon themselves the guilt for failures and unfulfilled dreams. The ageing king, turning more and more towards God after his Pyrrhic victories, needed a scapegoat in order to vindicate himself and do pleasing works in the eyes of his people. They, exhausted and wretched, needed a guilty party, a devil, someone to represent the root of all evil. Both found what they sought in the Protestants. As if following a recurrent law of social pressure, the hatred of the Catholic population and the punitive actions of the government were now directed more and more against these people, the group within their own country which seemed to them relatively the most alien.

Ideology and language, including official language, became increasingly violent. The king should do something for God was the first demand; he should protect the injured Mother Church, bind up the festering sore; later this was simplified to: 'France needs to be purged of all these monsters'. There was no ill that was not to be laid at the Protestants' door.

It began with the destruction of Protestant houses of prayer, with the forbidding of Huguenot clergy to call themselves 'pastor', with bureaucratic torments of every kind. As early as 1664 it had been decreed that only membership of the Catholic Church could be stated in licences granted to master craftsmen. But this decree had been somewhat neglected over time. Now its observance began to be strictly enforced. In 1679 a decree was published whereby Protestants were excluded from all offices in the service of large landowners; a decree of 1680 removed them from offices in the service of tax farmers; in the same year a ban on marriages between Catholics and Protestants was promulgated; in 1682 Protestants were denied entry to the profession of notary, and to any official activity at courts of law. This was followed by an influx of members of the reformed church to the so-called liberal professions. In Pau, for example, there were at that time 200 Protestant lawyers as compared to 50 Catholic. The result was a ban on the admission of Protestants to the legal profession. In 1685 they were denied admission to the medical profession, and involvement in all branches of the publishing, printing and bookselling trades.

In the first phase of the intensifying persecution of Protestants, it was still possible to believe the assertion that what was at issue was religion, and there is no doubt that some of the persecutors really believed that they were fighting to uphold the old true faith, and for purity of doctrine. Their aim, so they declared, was to force those of the RPR to abjure their errors. Rewards for conversion were promised. And, indeed, under the growing pressure more and more of them were converted. But this was not enough to meet the social objectives of the movement. The people needed guilty parties, scapegoats, human devils, to discharge their fury and assuage their distress. They wanted to be rid of competitors, to gain better social functions, to exploit the attendant opportunities for wealth and prestige; and when too many were converted, ostensibly or otherwise, for this purpose, finally no distinction was made between Protestant and recent convert. In terms of its social function, this religious persecution was a struggle of the majority against a minority which was economically and intellectually powerful but militarily weak, socially degraded and excluded from the apparatus of government. At a time when the population was increasing and the chances of satisfying the traditional standard of needs were growing fewer, this social function emerged in its nakedness.

This overt persecutory struggle was given special intensity by the influx of soldiers returning after the Treaties of Nijmegen. An army of 400,000 men, which up to then had been fed at least in part by war, returned to France. And if some of them soon found employment in new wars, the flow of old soldiers and officers nevertheless accelerated the process of expelling the Protestants; and the involvement in this process of those accustomed to pillaging, plundering and tormenting their fellow humans in every way set its special, characteristic stamp on the religious persecution.

It is, of course, hardly more than a coincidence that the 400,000 returning from the wars were matched by 300,000 Protestants who left the country. What is certain, however, is that the influx of these hundreds of thousands immensely increased the population pressure, and that old soldiers played a quite specific role in the persecution of Protestants. The historical symbol of the meeting between the mercenaries flooding back and the Protestants condemned to emigration are the infamous *dragonnades*.[3] The horror of this technique of persecution has tarnished forever the reputation of the reign of Louis XIV.

The wars of the seventeenth century were cruel in a somewhat different sense from those of today. The army had, as far as possible, to feed itself when on foreign soil. Plunder and rapine were not merely permitted,

3 *Dragonnades* – the billeting of troops in Protestant houses, used as a means of persecution.

but were demanded by military technique. To torment the subjugated inhabitants of occupied territories and to set fire to their houses – all this was, as well as a means of satisfying lust, a deliberate means of collecting war contributions and bringing to light concealed treasure. Soldiers were supposed to behave like robbers. It was banditry exacted and organised by the army commanders.

Grown accustomed to this life, the French mercenaries continued to behave in their own country, after the peace treaty, much as they had done previously on foreign soil. The Venetian ambassador wrote to his government at that time: 'I have with my own eyes seen small towns which previously had 700 or 800 dwellings but now, after the troops have passed through, have only thirty.' It was one of Louis XIV's provincial intendants who deliberately made use of this habit of the soldiery in the struggle against the Protestants. That was in 1680, one year after the Treaties had been concluded. Accompanied by monks and dragoons, he travelled through his province. The dragoons were billeted with Protestants. And they were allowed and obliged to abuse and beat their hosts as long as they refused to listen to the monks' sermons. What this meant is clear: women were dragged across the room by their hair, or with ropes; old people were tied to their beds and their children were mistreated before their eyes; people were made to sit on heated stoves; they were not allowed to sleep for days; the old soldiers were versed in torture of all kinds, indulging gladly in these practices in the name of the king and the affronted religion. An edict was issued: the billeted soldiers were to be copiously fed. In practice, this gave them the right to do and demand whatever they liked. To torture, rape and robbery were added economic ruin. The soldiers were ordered to create as much havoc as possible. The 'infernal legions' were allowed to commit any act short of direct murder; they could beat people, smoke them out, roast them, pour water into their mouths, make them dance till they fell, hang them by the nose or the toes – in a word: anything. Naturally, the king and his council had not directly and expressly ordered all this. 'It is possible', a historian writes, 'that they knew little of this; it is probable that they wished to know nothing'.[4]

The first *dragonnades* of 1680 had resulted immediately in 30,000 converts in one province. The great mass of Protestants still preferred to

4   The unnamed historian was probably Ernest Lavisse, whose *Louis XIV* is quoted by Elias early in the article. See p. 98, n. 1. The quotation from the Venetian ambassador from 1680 in the same paragraph may also have been taken from the same source.

live in their own country, even at the price of returning to the Catholic Church, rather than flee to a foreign land. The mass emigration of members of the reformed church began only when there was really no other possibility, no other protection for life and property. To begin with, only a trickle of Protestants, the especially fervent and obstinate ones, made their way secretly across the border.

But the more Protestants were converted so that they could stay at home, the less value their conversion had. Precisely because it was a mass conversion, the new converts formed a social group of their own. The Catholic Church was not able to digest them, clearly in part because at that time in France the Protestant clergy were superior to the Catholic in religious zeal, knowledge and power of conviction. For this very reason the Church urged the king to take a decisive step. The intendants, the judicial and administrative officials, and large sections of the Catholic population were also pushing, directly and indirectly, with various pretexts and for diverse practical reasons, in the same direction. In 1685 the king, inspired by his growing religious ardour and, above all, by a desire for absolute unity among his subjects, bowed to the general pressure and revoked the Edict of Nantes, thereby effectively revoking the equal rights of Protestants and of Protestant worship.

Central to the Edict of Revocation of the Edict was the expulsion of all Protestant priests from France, the destruction of the houses of prayer and a ban on Protestant worship and schools. Forced labour in the galleys was the penalty imposed for any infringement. But if the wording of the Revocation was directed primarily against clergy, worship and schools, in reality it intensified the terrible pressure already being exerted on *all* Protestants. It became a signal for a mass exodus.

The Revocation itself, of course, had prohibited emigration. For the king and his ministers, people as such counted as a piece of national wealth – which the energetic and commercially competent Protestants actually and especially were. But the social constellation, which from all sides strove for the expulsion of this section of society, was stronger than the will and intentions of its executors. Illegally, using a thousand disguises and stratagems, Protestant men, women and children migrated in huge numbers across the strictly guarded frontiers. Special organisations grew up to help the refugees and, if possible, their wealth, to leave the country. The king or his counsellors yielded in one of the decrees which followed: 'We do not wish', it stated, 'to prevent the Protestants from emigrating, but their wealth must stay in the country.' None of this made much difference to the secret border-crossing. Legally or illegally, about 200,000 French Protestants had left their homeland by 1685.

Their fate as emigrants is another story. At that time, the world was, economically, less interconnected than it is today. People of whom the economically overpopulated or – which comes to the same thing – the increasingly impoverished body politic of France had rid itself were, as we know, welcomed in other countries, especially Holland, Prussia, England, America and Switzerland. Louis XIV, who had hoped to annihilate Protestantism not only in France but in the whole of Europe, helped to spread and strengthen it.

The French who remained behind, however – or at least the great majority – suffered continuing poverty. These people who, unconsciously or half-consciously, had expected the extirpation of the Protestants to alleviate their misery, found themselves in no way better off. The king's financial policies, centrally determined by the desire for military power, for successful wars and for *gloire*, continued to burden the country. The state finances fell into increasing disorder. Poverty increased.

The connections between these phenomena can be discerned. The emigration of the Protestants from France is only an especially visible part of the wider social and economic process which the French social organism was undergoing at that time. In addition to the more or less consciously enforced Protestant emigration, there had already been a less visible Catholic one, as a simple consequence of the impoverishment of the country and of economic mismanagement. By 1720 a total of one million people, Catholic and Protestant, had emigrated from France.

But in France itself the ruinous financial policies led after the king's death to inflation and the concealed bankruptcy of the state. Moreover, as we know, the Protestants were never expelled entirely from France. Today they are again playing a not inconsiderable role, as they have for many years past. All the same, from the time of the Protestant emigration onwards, Catholicism has shaped the national character of France more clearly than before.

Appendix

The emergence of the modern natural sciences

Notes on the transcription

Reinhard Blomert discovered Norbert Elias's original typescript of the plan for his projected *Habilitation* thesis among Alfred Weber's papers in the University Library in Heidelberg, and transcribed it for publication as an appendix to his book *Intellektuelle im Aufbruch.* The text was reprinted in *Frühschriften,* the first volume of the Elias Collected Works in German.[1] In that volume, edited by Dr Blomert, the text is printed in a way that as nearly as possible reproduces the peculiarities of the appearance of the original typescript. Readers who are interested should consult the German edition. In this English edition, however, the intention has been, instead, to set out the document in such a way as to make the structure of Elias's research and his intended arguments as accessible as possible. The following notes are based on Dr Blomert's comments on the transcription in the *Frühschriften* volume, and upon his article 'Elias and Olschki'.[2]

Insertions made by Dr Blomert where there are gaps in the text resulting from physical damage to the original, or where the original formulation is incomplete, are indicated by square brackets in the English text; conjectural insertions by the German editor are indicated by a question mark within the square brackets.

Some not fully identified quotations occur in the text. '(O)' refers to Leonardo Olschki, and '(D)' to Pierre Duhem; these have been completed in square brackets in the transcription. Both authors were on the reading list for Alfred Weber's seminar on the Renaissance, in a section on the

1 Reinhard Blomert, *Intellektuelle im Aufbruch: Karl Mannheim, Alfred Weber, Norbert Elias und die Heidelberger Sozialwissenschaften der Zwischenkriegszeit* (Munich: Carl Hanser, 1999), pp. 351–64; reprinted in Norbert Elias, *Frühschriften,* Gesammelte Schriften, 1 (Frankfurt: Suhrkamp, 2002), pp. 86–102.

2 Reinhard Blomert, 'Hinweise zur Transkription', in Elias, *Frühschriften,* pp. 103–6; 'Elias and Olschki', *Figurations: Newsletter of the Norbert Elias Foundation* 6 (1996), p. 3.

subject of 'science and technology'.[3] Clearly legible on the reading list was the handwritten name 'N. Elias'.

In drawing up this *Habilitation* research proposal, Elias drew heavily on the work of Leonardo Olschki (1885–1961). Olschki, the son of a Jewish antiquarian from Florence, was Professor of Romance Philology at Heidelberg. A widely educated man, he had written a three-volume history of scientific literature in the modern languages, *Geschichte der neusprachliche wissensschaftliche Literatur*.[4] In this work, Olschki presents the thesis that the beginning of modern science could not evolve out of the scholastic university milieu. It developed rather in circles of practitioners – the *experimentierende Meister* – who were, as Elias stresses, at once craftsmen and artists. Elias points to the gap between the vertical, God-centred medieval thinking and the horizontal worldview of the rising epoch of the Renaissance, which for him represented a new stage in the history of thought.

Elias sometimes paraphrases Olschki's texts. Examples are lists such as the one of 'Brunelleschi's works' on p. 118, quoted in the same sequence as by Olschki (I, p. 43); on p. 121 the sequence of the members of the 'circle around Brunelleschi' (see Olschki, I, p. 33); the enumeration on p. 122, para. ?: 'Leonardo's notes . . .' with reference to Olschki (I, 286–7), where Olschki also writes, 'He [Leonardo] was on the way to determining that the moment of the results of two forces is equal to the sum of the moments of the components, . . .' (see p. 123 , 'He was close to recognising . . .'). Olschki refers here to Duhem, *Les origines de la statique*, I, p. 193, and Elias makes a similar reference to '(D)'.

The following passages are references to Olschki indicated by '(O)' or '(O.)':

On p. 121, regarding the 'education' of selected members of the circle: 'The most basic instruction . . .' The original quotation is as follows: 'They were all children of the people. They received the most basic instruction in reading, writing and arithmetic and began their artistic training while still in their childhood, with a goldsmith or woodcarver, and then tried their hand in all artistic genres until chance, their own aptitudes

---

3   For further details, see Blomert, *Intellektuelle im Aufbruch*, pp. 242 ff.

4   The three volumes are: I, *Die Literatur der Technik und der angewandten Wissenschaften vom Mittelalter bis zum Renaissance* (Heidelberg: Carl Winter, 1918); II, *Bildung und Wissenschaft in Zeitalter der Renaissance in Italien* (Florence: L. S. Olschkis Verlag, 1922); III, *Galilei und seine Zeit* (Halle: M. Niemeyer, 1924).

and routine limited their field of activity' (Olschki, I, pp. 33 ff.). What is significant is that Elias placed Olschki's term 'chance' in quotation marks.

On p. 122 Olschki is referred to again (point *(e)*, Leonardo da Vinci, Introduction, 2): 'The struggle for new forms of consciousness, for control of the natural world. Olschki wrong.' The quotation from Ghiberti which follows: 'Try with all means to imitate nature' appears in Olschki as follows: 'When Ghiberti was working on his masterwork he resolved, like every other artist of his time, 'to try with all means to imitate nature as far as possible' (Olschki, I, p. 263).

A direct quotation from Olschki appears on p. 123: 'Olschki:...'. The quotation ends with '... Critical examination of this opinion of Olschki's'. Olschki had written:

> In general, when biographers of Leonardo are asked why his forty years of intellectual activity yielded in this case only an unclear and timid approximation, they reply that the time was not yet ripe for the discovery of fundamental physical laws. But we shall not be content with such facile, fatalistic pronouncements.* The material available to Galileo's immediate predecessors a few decades later was not much more extensive and, above all, not significantly different to that used by Leonardo (Olschki, I, p. 294).

> * The history of physics teaches us that the results of the research of an individual are not duly acknowledged or understood or made use of by his contemporaries. But the discoveries are no less complete for that. Huygens's theory of light waves, which the great physicist had elaborated in the minutest detail in the mid-seventeenth century, was only understood and made use of in the nineteenth century. It was the same with the discoveries of a Pascal, a Mariotte and other researchers. The delayed effect of their teachings depends on circumstances and on the interests and needs of human beings. [Olschki's footnote].

On several occasions in the second volume of his trilogy, Olschki mentions the historian of science Pierre Duhem (1861–1916). In footnote 2, p. 41, Olschki writes: 'Relations with Leonardo da Vinci are discussed extensively in Duhem, *Origines de la statique*, vol. I, pp. 194 ff., vol. II, pp. 380 f.; also *Études sur Léonard da Vinci*, Third series, 1913, pp. 186 ff., by the same author.'[5] Again, on p. 49, he writes, 'In recent decades historians of the mathematical sciences, such as Vailati, Wohlwill, Caverni and Duhem

---

5   Pierre Duhem, *Les origins de la statique*, 2 vols (Paris: A. Hermann, 1905–6); *Études sur Léonard da Vinci*, 3rd ser., *Les précurseurs parisens de Galilée* (Paris: A. Hermann, 1913).

have polemicised against Lagrange who, in the historical introduction to his *Mécanique analitique,* hardly acknowledged Galileo's precursors as such, so that Galileo's work could be presented in splendid isolation.'

The emergence of the modern natural sciences: plan

Introduction

The initial constellation of the modern age is at the same time the final constellation of the Middle Ages. Natural science is only *one* expression of a new mental-spiritual attitude of Western people.

In order not only to describe the emergence of this new attitude from the outside, but to make it understandable from the inside, the following are necessary:

1   Exploration of the way in which the non-enlightened person, the medieval person, experienced what we call 'Nature'.

2   Exploration of the external and internal trends through which this medieval way of experiencing the physical world gradually changed.

3   Supercession of the self-evidence of our experience of the physical world as 'Nature' and emphasis on what is new, unique and physiognomically significant in this experience.

1   In what way did the medieval person experience the cosmos as it could be perceived with the senses?

A. Material
2 examples. Both from the world of priests and scholars. More influential than today for the experience of *all* people.

Plan of Norbert Elias's projected *Habilitation* thesis to be supervised by Alfred Weber. First published in Reinhart Blomert, *Intellektuelle im Aufbruch: Karl Mannheim, Alfred Weber, Norbert Elias und die Heidelberger Sozialwissenschaften der Zwischenkriegszeit* (Munich: Carl Hanser, 1999) pp. 351–64 (Appendix).

a) Dietrich v. Freiberg (Theodoricus Teutonicus)[1]

Early 14th century. Explanation of the rainbow. Probable sources apart from Aristotle: Al-Farisi[2] and other Arabs.

Characteristic of him: transcribing incorrect numbers from the sources and casual use of them. Hardly any conclusions from his own observations. Example of his method: Question about the principles by which four colours were produced by sunlight striking cloud. Answer: 2 more formal and 2 more material principles, something transparent of greater brightness and something transparent of lesser brightness, something firmly delimited and something less firmly delimited [or] not delimited firmly at all. As water, fire, air and earth originate from the mixture of warm, cold, moist and dry (Aristotle!), 4 colours originate from the mixture of those 4 principles. *Principle* as *cause of the emergence of colours* (such as . . .) Not to observe, but to learn from books the *names* of the *substantiae formales* from which something originates, was the goal of researchers. The spiritual nature of the *substantiae*. The way of communicating with God [as] communication of a spiritual being with spiritual beings. Revelation, not rational cognition of truth. Books!

b) The word 'natura' as used by Saint Thomas[3]

Not mechanically lawlike entity, which stands opposed to everything intellectual and spiritual as something different, but precisely this principle generates all that is living or spiritual (*nasci*)

> *At the centre of what is expressed by the medieval term 'natura' is not rock or the stars, but the human being and God.*

Evidence: the Thomist concept of '*lex naturalis*'

Not abstract, mathematically expressible regularity but

1   Dietrich von Freiberg (1250–1310): sometimes known as Theodoricus Teutonicus, a German Dominican scholar of philosophy, theology and natural science, known particularly for his treatises on light and colour which contributed to the development of optics. Elias refers to his work on rainbows, which was contained in his treatise *De iride*. See Dietrich von Freiberg, *On the Rainbow: A Source Book in Medieval Science*, ed. Edward Grant (Cambridge, MA: Harvard University Press, 1974).

2   Al-Farisi (*c.*1260–1320): also known as Kamal al-din, a Persian scholar of mathematics who developed a testable theory of refraction to explain the colours of the rainbow. See Carl B. Boyer, *The Rainbow: From Myth to Mathematics* (New York: T. Yoseloff, 1959).

3   St Thomas Aquinas (1225–74): developed the concept of *lex naturalis* (natural law), to which Elias refers in the text, in his *Summa Theologiae*.

1   *The striving for the good, for perfection* (also applies to rocks!)

2   *Everything by which the human being preserves life.*

(Eating, digesting, concourse of the sexes and *education of children*)

3   Just as the inclination towards goodness is in accord with the nature of reason, so also is *the inclination to discover truth from God, to avoid ignorance and not to offend others*)

Verbatim from St Thomas!

This detailed treatment is important, as it is necessary to understand the old in order to understand the new.

Pay attention to this question: The way in which the physical world is experienced. Reference to alchemy, astrology, witches etc.

How was it experienced? *Not as Nature!*

c)   Overall vision of the shape taken by the world for the consciousness of medieval people

1   *Realm of spirits centred on God and man. Hierarchy* (angel, man, plant, animal, reference to the polity of estates)

2   *Every motion the emanation of a spiritual will*

3   Communication between beings in the same way as between spirits

4   Revelation, knowledge from books written by people inspired by grace

Reality of the word (as cause, magic, invocation)

5   Authoritarian thinking. (A word, a concept which is found in ancient writings (the transparent – of brighter clarity, elucidated)

2   *In the course of which movements and conflicts was the dominance of the authoritarian world picture shaken, broken and slowly replaced by a new worldview?*

Introduction

The medieval soul and spirit have clear and fixed physiognomies. Absurd to believe that their bearers are by nature different from us, and that a new nature has arrived, people of greater intelligence or genius than the Scholastics. *Genius and spiritual-social movement.*

a)   Sociological centre of the dominant medieval education
The universities
Monopoly of knowledge of the world. Sins could be forgiven, heresies which undermined the traditional world picture were punished with fire and sword. Necessity of this tie. Error of the Enlightenment's condemnation of this attitude.

Means of denying laypeople the ability to judge this knowledge of the world:

> *The Latin language*
> *Copernicus* tolerated in Latin, *Galileo* forced to recant in the language of the populace.

> *Republic of scholars*
> The fate of Galileo, condemned because he stepped outside the circle of *scholars* and addressed a wide lay audience, showing with [...] force the *constellation in which the new way of* [seeing] *nature came into being: the new established itself in the struggle against the university and against the Latin language.* By whom was this struggle against the scholars waged?

b)[4]   *The uneducated,* the people who had not passed through the Latin School, the laypeople, *practical men. One could not learn from books alone that there might be another way of attaining certainty than through books.* The idea of observing, of being able to discover truth by observing, measuring and weighing, was not self-evident. Its self-evidence should be understood as something which has become problematic.

   The new could not come into being in just any social stratum. Specific experiences and knowledge were necessary.

Social movement and mental-spiritual movement identical
Craftsmen, artists, engineers. Nothing about superstructure and base, nothing about ideology.[5] Let us look at the facts.

---

   4   Here Elias went from subsection *a)* to one numbered 2 rather than *b)*; this has been changed to clarify the structure of his notes.
   5   A reference to the Marxian theory of historical materialism, which Elias had clearly abandoned as a useful framework for the research. The previous remarks in the text indicate that one of the reasons for his rejection was its dualistic character. Elias returns to this weakness in Marx's theory several times in his later essays on the sociology of knowledge and science written in the 1970s and 1980s (to be published in vol. 14 of the Collected Works).

3   Materials on the sociology of the emergent natural science

a)   Political-historical constellation

Decline in the strength of the central state authority in the Holy Roman Empire, especially in Italy, after Rudolph von Habsburg. Henry VII is able to settle the factional struggles in Milan, is welcomed in Genoa and Pisa, but is unable to capture Florence. *The city triumphs over the Emperor.* 1313.

No less weak was the *central spiritual authority.* 1309 Clement V to Avignon. From 1378 two popes. Unity was not restored until the Council of Konstanz, 1414–18.

The weakness of the centripetal forces[6] *was the precondition for the expanding power of the centrifugal ones, the princes and cities.*

Princes not to be discussed here, nor Lübeck nor Nuremberg. Nevertheless, victory of the Swabian cities over the Count of Württemberg in 1377.

Florence

A rich, economically powerful, politically and socially independent and self-confident middle class. Through control of the countryside the citizens gradually supplant a prince (Tuscany, capture of Pisa 1429). The rich banker Giovanni de' Medici becomes the representative of this domination. *Guildsmen, merchants and craftsmen rule over an entire territory, banker's family becomes a dynasty of princes.*

That is the *intellectual and social atmosphere* in which the development under discussion here took place.

Two circles	1	Experimenting master craftsmen
	2	Platonic academy
		Representatives of the Renaissance

---

6   The concepts of centripetal and centrifugal forces were later to be used extensively by Elias in *The Civilising Process* in his model of waves of centralising and decentralising forces in the power figuration of medieval society which led to the formation of modern states. See Norbert Elias, *The Civilising Process: Sociogenetic and Psychogenetic Investigations*, trans. Edmund Jephcott, one-volume revised edition by Eric Dunning, Johan Goudsblom and Stephen Mennell (Oxford: Blackwell, 2000; original publication in German, 1939), especially Part Three, and the further revised edition of this text to appear as vol. 3 of the Collected Works.

b)   The circle of experimenting master craftsmen

Introduction

Quite certainly *not the first* to carry out observations on the properties and behaviour of bodies in the service of human purposes. *Difference*: Knowledge was stored in the tradition; more or less *accidental* discoveries were accumulated and passed on from the *master to the apprentice*. Now something new: *the acquisition of knowledge through deliberate observation, experience and reflection*. In short, through *experiments*.

However, all this initially in the service of human purposes!

Not yet science as we understand it, but the first step towards the revolution in the medieval world picture.

1   Comparison of *Giotto and Masaccio*

a)   Giotto[7] the pious pupil of the medieval-ecclesiastical tradition, in depicting which his creative powers unfold. *No distinction between man and nature*. World/*kingdom of God*, at the centre of which stands man.

The *illusion* that what is represented is taking place here and now before the onlooker is still very unimportant to him. What is crucial is the *spiritual* relationship of the onlooker to what is represented. The beauty and greatness of his paintings stem from the fervour with which he portrays a spiritual content. The formal beauty a development of the traditional inheritance rather than a product of conscious reflection on colours and lines and their harmony, their proportions.

The survival of the Gothic-scholastic tradition, to which Giotto gave magnificent expression, as empty schooling even a century later, at the time of the experimenting masters. *Gentile da Fabriano*. The figure without mass, the body without muscles, linear arabesques.

---

7   Giotto di Bondone (*c.*1267–1337): Florentine painter and architect widely regarded the first genius of art in the Italian Renaissance. In the remainder of the document, Elias cites or refers to a number of other Italian painters, sculptors, architects, scientists and philosophers. In the order of their occurrence in the text these are: Tommaso Masaccio (1401–28); Gentile da Fabriano (*c.*1370–1427); Filippo Brunelleschi (1377–1446); Paolo Uccello (1396–1475); Luca della Robbia (*c.*1400–82); Leon Battista Alberti (1404–72); Donatello (*c.*1386–1466); Lorenzo Ghiberti (1378–1455); Paolo dal Pozzo Toscanelli (1398–1482); Marsilio Ficino (also known as Marsilius Ficinus, the name by which Elias cites him) (1433–99); Leonardo da Vinci (1452–1519); Giordano Bruno (1548–1600); and Galileo Galilei (1564–1642). Elias returned to the question of the connection between scientific and artistic developments in the Introduction to a later work, *Involvement and Detachment* (Oxford: Basil Blackwell, 1987); a revised edition of this book will appear as vol. 8 of the Collected Works. There he mentions again the significance of the Florentine painters in the Italian Renaissance and refers to some of those cited above.

b)   Masaccio, from the circle of experimenting masters around Brunelleschi
The new attitude to the image is at the same time an expression of the different religiosity of a different stance towards the world. Tendency towards independence from tradition. Think through for yourself what is handed down. An attitude which in Germany leads to Luther (reception above all at economic centres, in cities), in Florence to Savonarola.

Body and action are no longer symbols intended to awaken memories of something transcendent in the onlooker. Masaccio wants to represent events *as if they were taking place here and now before the onlooker.* New *realistic, unscholarly, unscholastic attitude* to matters of faith and the world.

New attitude identical to new tasks
In the circle around Brunelleschi to which Masaccio belonged the new task was formulated as follows: Things were to be painted *as if one were viewing what is represented through a window.* This task could not be performed solely with traditional painting technique, with practices and experiences that had been handed down. One had to *experiment.*

The new task: How must the actual proportions of things be changed to make them appear in the two-dimensional picture plane as if they were located in three-dimensional space?

A genuine problem of construction: an exercise in the field of representational geometry. The struggle for this in the work of Masaccio.

The man who solved this problem – and solved it by experimenting, calculating observing, by drawings, technical aids, etc. – was the centre of the circle of experimenting masters, Brunelleschi.

c)   Filippo Brunelleschi 1377–1446
Craftsman without Latin education. Architect and engineer. No misunderstanding if one has so much to do with artists and technicians. From the research and experiments in the service of human purposes there gradually arose that disposition of consciousness, that mental–spiritual constellation, those modes of thought, which gave rise to research and experimentation without any 'purpose' for human beings other than what they now called 'truth'. A new time, a new social atmosphere set new tasks.

The tendency to reproduce things realistically in paintings was not the only new task. Artists engaged in profane tasks much more than earlier, in conjunction with the consolidation of civic prosperity. New social atmosphere identical to new spiritual atmosphere –

Brunelleschi's works: (selection)
Erection of fortifications at Pisa and Vico Pisano
fortresses in the Elsa Valley
Regulation of the Arno
Construction of Po embankments
Design of harbour fortifications at Rimini
Execution of the dome of Florence Cathedral (39 m)
Palazzi

Demands of civil and military technology. New problems of statics, hydraulics and ballistics, not to be solved *by technical routine alone but by tests and theoretical reflection.*

Construction of new machines; combined levers and inclined planes for the dome structure in Florence.

N.B.: The problem of inclined planes first exercises minds as a problem in the service of human purposes. Only gradually, first of all in Galileo, does it become a problem of the non-purposive cognition of nature. Here one may have an inkling of how the new human attitude, and the new idea of natural laws, grew up very slowly in the work of human beings on temporal–spatial materials.

The growth of the idea of a calculable regularity exempt from all arbitrariness as, at the same time, a regularity of nature and a regularity of works of art, in an inseparable unity. At first, no distinction between these two regularities in the Renaissance. *Brunelleschi must be understood in this way.*

Just as, *with the intuition of a genius,* he tested, and reflected on, the regularity of things in constructing bridges and fortifications, in the same way he tested and reflected on the regularity, the harmony and proportions of buildings.

He was thus the first to formulate the rules of a *proportione armonica* according to which buildings must be built. 1403–4

Renaissance art and Renaissance science
are offspring of one and the same human attitude

Example: Perspective
(already mentioned above regarding Masaccio)

Question (as formulated above): In painting, how must the actual proportions of things be changed to make them appear in the two-dimensional picture plane as if they were located in three-dimensional space?

Devices constructed by Brunelleschi to solve this problem (mirrors). The construction of the vanishing lines of a picture leading towards a point was, relatively, the simplest task. Much more difficult – and especially characteristic of the questions which exercised the time – was *the solution to the problem of how sizes decrease in the picture in accordance with distance.* In the preceding period, and even among B's contemporaries, a type of representation in which distances, seen from the onlooker's viewpoint, appear too short, lead upwards too quickly. The specific *abstraction* demanded by the new task: The painter had to construct the picture so that it appeared to lead into depth in a perspectively correct way, not directly for him but for the viewer standing at a certain distance from the picture plane. Specific geometrical construction necessary for this.

Brunelleschi discovered this construction. The idea of calculable pictorial harmony and the idea of calculable natural laws were inseparable at the moment of birth. New human sense of happiness, new method of creating art, new attitude of the artist to his work, new attitude of the human being to the cosmos of what is perceptible to the senses.

Immersion in the religious content of what is depicted gives way to immersion behind the regularity and harmony of what is perceptible to the senses.

Uccello (also from the circle of experimenting masters):
'*How sweet a thing is perspective*'

We shall see, perhaps, how the exponents of this new feeling of life finally came into conflict with the exponents of the old sacred authorities founded on revelation.

Summary
D[uhem][8]

1   *The painting as illusion* (convergence of realistic and illusionistic painting. Reminder of theatre as an element of the Renaissance).
2   *The painting as a beautiful, i.e. regular form*
       (Autonomy of the beautiful. What is represented recedes behind the representation)

8   See pp. 107–10 above.

3   *Experiment and mathematical calculation as means of discovering regularities in nature and art*
(No separation of knowledge of nature from feeling for nature; feeling and *ratio,* soul and mind still one)

4   *This manner of orienting oneself in the chaos of material things by experimentation and calculation = the idea of natural science*
Question: Where did these 'uneducated' people acquire their knowledge of mathematics?

d)   Connection between the experimenting masters and the Latin tradition
The real problem of the Renaissance for culture sociology
Introduction

In the circle of the experimenting masters a new human attitude had achieved clear expression for the first time, and for the first time was *given shape* by them. Earlier, the knights had fashioned a specifically 'knightly' education from the attitude and forms conferred on them by their specific function as 'knights', and the priests and scholars created a specific education on the basis of their specific functions. In the same way, the experimenting masters, freed from the authority of other strata, began for the first time to develop – directly from their professional activity, their specific functions – a civic society, the society of the merchants and craftsmen of Florence. They began to develop a very specific education, specific art, specific forms of knowledge, expressed in a specific language only now elevated to the medium of education. That – from the perspective of Western education as a whole – was a revolution. But there are no absolute revolutions. In some form the old cultural heritage was incorporated in the new form of education, partly determining its physiognomy.

Specific phenomenon of the Renaissance: the collaboration of certain scholars, the bearers of the old, Latin educational tradition, with the experimenting masters, the bearers of the new. But the vessel into which Latin education now flowed, the circle of artists and architects, was different from all previous circles which had adopted and carried forward Latin education. The way in which antiquity was experienced [and] given shape here was different from the way it had been given form by the scholars who lacked any relationship to living practice, the humanists and scholastics. For the first time antiquity was no longer the authority but the great teacher, whose teaching could be tested and further developed on the basis of one's own experience.

1   Social origins and education of the circle around Brunelleschi
     Philippo Brunelleschi, Luca della Robbia, Masaccio, Alberti,
        Donatello, Ghiberti, etc.
                Time: Brunelleschi 1377–1446
                           Alberti b. 1407
                           Ghiberti 1380–1455[9]

Origins: Details uncertain; at any rate from the less well to do lower stratum
or the middle classes, apart from A[lberti].

Education: The most basic instruction in reading, writing and arithmetic;
training with wood-carver or goldsmith while still in childhood. Tried
their hands at all genres of art until 'chance', personal aptitude and
routine limited their field of activity (O[lschki]).[10] No knowledge of Latin.
No mathematics. The arithmetic books of the 15th and 16th centuries,
written in the language of the populace, met only the most basic practical
requirements.

Paradox: The scholars who understood Latin had no direct access to the
material world, and what the ancient authors say about the material world
was for them just as much an authoritarian doctrine as the teachings of the
Church authorities.

   On the other hand, the artists, craftsmen and technicians, who might
have been able to understand the ancient teachings in their original sense,
did not understand Latin.

   Stimulation of craft and technical work by antiquity through the
collaborative friendship of scholars and artists.

1   *Brunelleschi and Toscanelli* (b. 1396, i.e. 22 years younger than
     B[runelleschi].[11])
2   Alberti, Leon Battista (biography, uniqueness of Florence, switched
from scholar to practitioner)
     Comparison with humanism (Ficinus)

9 Elias cited Lorenzo Ghiberti's date of birth wrongly as 1380. It was in fact 1378.
10 See pp. 107–10 above.
11 Elias cited Paolo dal Pozzo Toscanelli's date of birth wrongly as 1396. It was in fact 1398.

e) Leonardo da Vinci

Introduction: Fifty years later. New constellation in Florence. Spread of Brunelleschi's tradition across the Apennines. In Florence scholarship and living practice once again separate to some extent

1   Biography (uncertainty)

2   The struggle for new forms of consciousness, for control of the natural world. Olschki wrong.

Ghiberti already quoted as saying: Try with all means to imitate nature. Now, with Leonardo, observation (conscious observation!) across the whole breadth of the natural world. The loneliness of the great men (reference to Bruno, Galileo, Copernicus)

Leonardo's wrestling with the category of *mechanical* causation. Still no definitive break with the medieval categories. This was the problem of his life, the difficulty facing his understanding.

Leitmotif: Observation, contempt for all erudition that goes beyond observation.

3   Necessity of the stage that Leonardo represents for us: comparison with the development of the discipline of history. First, the collection of an abundance of materials. Everything is new. Mastering of the collected material by an ordering principle is only a further stage. Man is slowly displaced from the centre of the 'concept of nature' [and] begins to become what he is for the Enlightenment: one body among others, subject to the single all-embracing regularity

Examples. Observation of the mechanisms of bodily movements in human beings and animals, anatomical, physiological investigations of the [?] Only seeing can unravel the secrets of nature. Therefore, something can often the expressed by drawings that can be less well expressed in words.

Leonardo's notes on all natural phenomena – which he observed not only as a landscape painter but as a technician, in designing and executing canals, river regulation projects, roads, dams, bridges, locks, fortifications – are full of descriptions, analyses, calculations, drawings.

Apart from fauna, flora, bodies of water, rocks and grottoes, he is always fascinated by the most fantastical things, by mystery. (O[lschki])

He, too, moved from artistic and technical practice to non-purposive observation, from 'curiosity' about mystery. (O[lschki])

Characteristic plans: encyclopaedia of technology for theory and practice

Grammar of the popular language.

However, he always confines himself to single observations and never achieves a systematic synthesis. He was close to recognising that the moment of the results of two forces is equal to the sum of the moments of the components, and similarly in many other cases (D[uhem]). But he never took the step from experience to pure abstraction in the form of laws.

Olschki: In general, when biographers of Leonardo are asked why his forty years of intellectual activity yielded in this case (in relation to laws) only unclear and timid answers, they reply that the time was not yet ripe for the discovery of fundamental physical laws. But we shall not be content with such facile, fatalistic pronouncements. The material available to Galileo's immediate predecessors a few decades later was not much more extensive and, above all, not significantly different from that used by Leonardo.

Critical examination of this opinion of Olschki's.

Summary
What was the new thinking that grew up at that time?

From the idea of the spiritual realm there arose, as autonomous spheres of being, the idea of beauty and the idea of nature as aspects of the world, subject to laws of their own. The idea of the authorship of all existing things by one spiritual being was replaced by the idea of mechanical causation calculable on the basis of laws. The gaining of certainty on the basis of revelation, whose vessel was the authoritarian books, was replaced by the gaining of certainty on the basis of one's own un-authoritarian observations and reflections.

And so, as always after a spiritual revolution, humankind was endowed with a new joy and a new sorrow. The new joy that the consciousness of their own powers of cognition gave to human beings, and the new sorrow: the suffering born of this very consciousness, the chill sobriety of the individual's power of cognition, or rationality.

Bibliography

Works to which Elias makes reference

Bernhard, Ludwig, *Der Hugenbergkonzern* (Berlin: J. Springer, 1928).

Cassirer, Ernst, *Kants Leben und Lehre* (Berlin: Bruno Cassirer, 1918); trans. James Haden as *Kant's Life and Thought* (New Haven CT: Yale University Press, 1991).

Duhem, Pierre, *Les Origines de la statique*, 2 vols (Paris: A. Hermann, 1905–6).

Duhem, Pierre, *Études sur Léonard da Vinci*, 3rd ser., *Les Précurseurs parisiens de Galilée* (Paris: A. Hermann, 1913).

Kant, Immanuel, *The Critique of Pure Reason* (1781), trans. and ed. Paul Guyer and Allen W. Wood (Cambridge: Cambridge University Press, 1998).

Kant, Immanuel, *The Critique of Practical Reason* (1788), trans. Lewis White Beck (Indianapolis: Liberal Arts Press, 1956).

Kant, Immanuel, *The Critique of Judgement* (1790), trans. Werner S. Pluhar (Indianapolis: Hackett, 1987).

Lavisse, Ernest, *Louis XIV: La fronde, Le roi, Colbert (1643–85)* (Paris: Hachette, 1907) [vol. VII, part 1 of Lavisse (ed.), *Histoire de France: depuis les origines jusqu'à la révolution*, 9 vols (Paris: Hachette, 1900–11)].

Mahraum, Artur, *Das jungdeutsche Manifest: Volk gegen Kaste und Geld* (Berlin: Jungdeutscher Verlag, 1927).

Mannheim, Karl 'Competition as a cultural phenomenon', in Karl Mannheim, *Essays on the Sociology of Knowledge*, ed. Paul Kecskemeti (London: Routledge & Kegan Paul, 1952 [1928]), pp. 191–229.

Olschki, Leonardo, *Geschichte der neusprachliche wissensschaftliche Literatur*. 3 vols: I, *Die Literatur der Technik und der angewandten Wissenschaften vom Mittelalter bis zum Renaissance* (Heidelberg: Carl Winter, 1918); II, *Bildung und Wissenschaft in Zeitalter der Renaissance in Italien* (Florence: L. S. Olschkis Verlag, 1922); III, *Galilei und seine Zeit* (Halle: M. Niemeyer).

Works to which editorial reference is made

Arrian [Lucius Flavius Arrianus], *History of Alexander and Indica*, trans. P. A. Brunt, 2 vols (Cambridge MA: Harvard University Press, 1983).

Blomert, Reinhard, 'Elias and Olschki', *Figurations: Newsletter of the Norbert Elias Foundation* 6 (1996), p. 3.

Bogner, Artur, 'Elias and the Frankfurt School', *Theory, Culture and Society* 4:2–3 (1987), pp. 249–85.

Elias, Norbert, *The Civilising Process: Sociogenetic and Psychogenetic Investigations*, trans. Edmund Jephcott, rev. Eric Dunning, Johan Goudsblom and Stephen Mennell (Oxford: Blackwell, 2000 [orig. in German, 1939]). Collected Works, vol. 3, *On the Process of Civilisation*.

Elias, Norbert, *Involvement and Detachment* (Oxford: Basil Blackwell, 1987). Collected Works, vol. 8.

Elias, Norbert, *Los der Menschen: Gedichte/Nachdichtungen* (Frankfurt am Main, Suhrkamp, 1988).

Elias, Norbert, *The Symbol Theory*, ed. Richard Kilminster (London: Sage, 1991). Collected Works, vol. 13.

Elias, Norbert, *Mozart: Portrait of a Genius*, ed. Michael Schröter (Cambridge: Polity, 1993). Collected Works, vol. 12, *Mozart: On the Sociology of a Genius*.

Elias, Norbert, *Reflections on a Life*, trans. Edmund Jephcott (Cambridge: Polity, 1994). Collected Works, vol. 17.

Elias, Norbert, *The Germans: Power Struggles and the Development of Habitus in the Nineteenth and Twentieth Centuries*, trans. Eric Dunning and Stephen Mennell, ed. Michael Schröter (Cambridge: Polity, 1996). Collected Works, vol. 11, *Studies on the Germans*.

Elias, Norbert and Eric Dunning, *Quest for Excitement: Sport and Leisure in the Civilising Process* (Oxford, Basil Blackwell, 1986). Collected Works, vol. 7.

Goudsblom, Johan, *Sociology in the Balance* (Oxford: Blackwell, 1977).

Goudsblom, Johan and Stephen Mennell (eds), *The Norbert Elias Reader: A Biographical Selection* (Oxford: Blackwell, 1998).

Köhnke, Klaus Christian, *The Rise of Neo-Kantianism: German Academic Philosophy between Idealism and Positivism*, trans. R. J. Hollingdale (Cambridge: Cambridge University Press, 1991).

Kuzmics, Helmut, 'Bibliographical retrospect: Julius Stenzel, *Philosophie der Sprache*, Munich and Berlin, Oldenbourg Verlag, 1934', *Figurations: Newsletter of the Norbert Elias Foundation* 15 (2001), p. 14.

Lévy-Bruhl, Lucien, *How Natives Think*, trans. Lilian A. Clare (Princeton, NJ: Princeton University Press, 1985 [1910]).

Lévy-Bruhl, Lucien, *Primitive Mentality*, trans. Lilian A. Clare (Boston: Beacon, 1966).

Mann, Klaus, *The Turning Point: Thirty-Five Years in This Century: The Autobiography of Klaus Mann* (New York: Markus Wiener, 1984 [1942]).

Mannheim, Karl, 'Conservative thought', in Karl Mannheim, *Essays on Sociology and Social Psychology*, ed. Paul Kecskemeti (London: Routledge & Kegan Paul, 1953), pp. 74–164. [This essay was drawn from Mannheim's Heidelberg *Habilitationsschrift*, which was examined in December 1925; the *venia legendi* or licence to teach was awarded on 12 June 1926. The essay 'Das konservative Denken: Soziologische Beiträge zum Werden des Politisch-historischen Denkens in Deutschland' was published over two issues of the *Archiv für Sozialwissenschaft und Sozialpolitik*, LVII:1 (1927), pp. 68–142; 2 (1927), pp. 47–95. The English 'Conservative thought' contains additional materials from the *Habilitationsschrift*.]

Mannheim, Karl, *Conservatism: A Contribution to the Sociology of Knowledge*, ed. David Kettler, Volker Meja and Nico Stehr (London: Routledge & Kegan Paul, 1986).

Meja, Volker and Nico Stehr (eds), *Knowledge and Politics: The Sociology of Knowledge Dispute* (London: Routledge, 1990).

Plato, *The Republic*, trans. Paul Shorey, 12 vols (Cambridge MA: Harvard University Press, 1930).

Plutarch, *Lives*, trans. B. Perrin, 11 vols (Cambridge MA: Harvard University Press, 1914).

Schiller, Friedrich von, *Naïve and Sentimental Poetry, and On the Sublime: Two Essays, Friedrich von Schiller*, trans and ed. Julius A. Elias (New York: F. Ungar, 1966).

Stenzel, Julius, *Philosophie der Sprache* (Munich and Berlin, Oldenbourg Verlag, 1934).

Taine, Hyppolite, *Les Origines de la France contemporaine*, 3 vols (Paris: Hachette, 1878–92).

Weber, Alfred, 'Fundamentals of culture sociology: social process, civilisational process and culture-movement', trans. G. H. Weltner and C. F. Hirshman, Department of Social Science, Columbia University, 1939 [orig. in *Archiv für Sozialwissenschaft und Sozialpolitik* 47 (1920–1), pp. 1–49; reprinted in John Rundell and Stephen Mennell (eds), *Classical Readings in Culture and Civilisation* (London: Routledge, 1998), pp. 191–215.]

Wolin, Richard, *Heidegger's Children: Hannah Arendt, Karl Löwith, Hans Jonas, and Herbert Marcuse* (Princeton, NJ: Princeton University Press, 2003).

Relevant additional references

Berkowitz, Michael, *Western Jewry and the Zionist Project, 1914–1933* (Cambridge: Cambridge University Press, 1996).

Brenner, Michael, *The Renaissance of Jewish Culture in Weimar Germany* (New Haven, CT: Yale University Press, 1996).

Crowell, Steven Galt, 'Neo-Kantianism', in Simon Critchley and William R. Schroeder (eds), *A Companion to Continental Philosophy* (Oxford: Blackwell, 1999), pp. 185–97.

Gay, Peter, *Weimar Culture: The Outsider as Insider* (Harmondsworth: Penguin, 1974).

Goudsblom, Johan, 'Responses to Norbert Elias's work in England, Germany, the Netherlands and France', in Peter Gleichmann, Johan Goudsblom and Hermann Korte (eds), *Human Figurations: Essays for Norbert Elias* (Amsterdam: Stichting Amsterdams Sociologisch Tijdschrift, 1977), pp. 37–97.

Hackeschmidt, Jörg, 'Norbert Elias – Zionist and *Bündisch* activist', *Figurations: Newsletter of the Norbert Elias Foundation* 3 (1995), pp. 4–5.

Kilminster, Richard, 'Editor's introduction', in Norbert Elias, *The Symbol Theory* (London: Sage, 1991).

Kilminster, Richard, 'Norbert Elias and Karl Mannheim: closeness and distance', *Theory, Culture and Society* 10:3 (1993), pp. 81–114.

Kilminster, Richard and Cas Wouters, 'From philosophy to sociology: Elias and the Neo-Kantians: a response to Benjo Maso', *Theory, Culture and Society* 12:3 (1995), pp. 81–120.

Mannheim, Karl, 'German sociology (1918–1933)', in Karl Mannheim, *Essays on the Sociology and Social Psychology*, ed. Paul Kecskemeti (London: Routledge & Kegan Paul, 1953 [1934]), pp. 209–28.

Maso, Benjo, 'Elias and the Neo-Kantians: intellectual backgrounds of *The Civilising Process*', *Theory, Culture and Society* 12:3 (1995), pp. 43–79.

Mennell, Stephen, *Norbert Elias: An Introduction* (Dublin: University College Dublin Press, 1998).

Mennell, Stephen, 'Another biographical footnote: Elias and St Edith Stein', *Figurations: Newsletter of the Norbert Elias Foundation* 19 (2003), p. 6.

Mosse, George L., *Germans and Jews: The Right, the Left and the Search for a 'Third Force' in Pre-Nazi Germany* (Detroit: Wayne State University Press, 1987).

Rabinbach, Anson, *In the Shadow of Catastrophe: German Intellectuals between Apocalypse and Enlightenment* (Berkeley, University of California Press, 1997).

Index